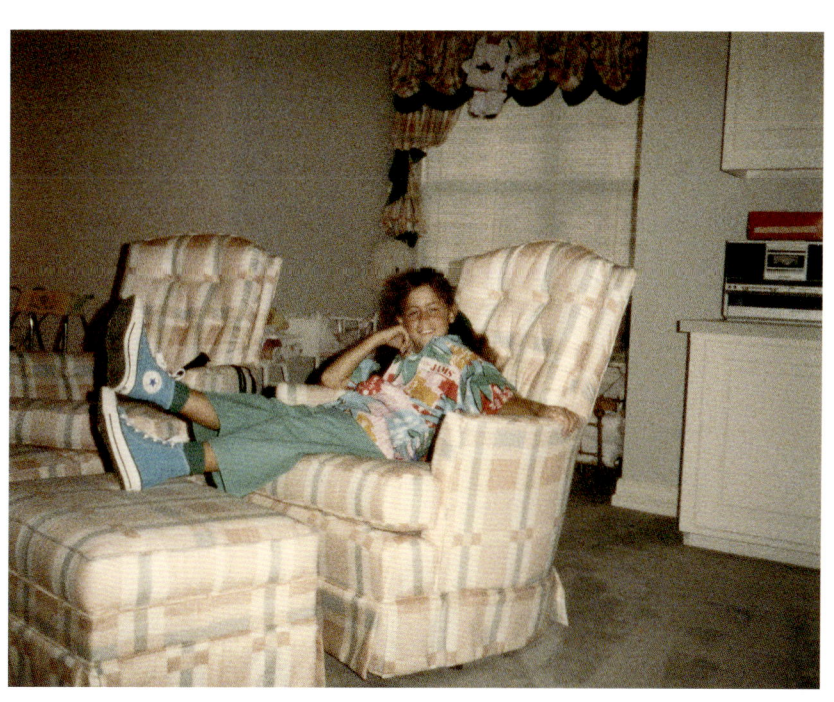

Daylight

# Stories
# 1986-88

Diane Durant

Cofounders: Taj Forer and Michael Itkoff
Creative Director: Ursula Damm
Copy Editor: Barbara Richard

© 2020 Daylight Community Arts Foundation

Photographs © 2020 by Diane Durant

The Difficult Business of Being Human © 2020 by Diane Durant
Foreword © 2020 by Dr. Sheree Gallager, Psy.D.
Afterword © 2020 by Andie McGurren

ISBN: 978-1-942084-77-8

Printed in China by Artron

Daylight Books
info@daylightbooks.org
www.daylightbooks.org

For my daughter, who can be whomever she wants to be

(now that she's no longer being me)

# FOREWORD

## by Dr. Sheree Gallagher, Psy.D.

Childhood is a precious time. Carefree and full of dreams, we learn something new every day. It is also a time of significant development that occurs across periods of both exponential growth and slow progression as we learn about ourselves and others. Vulnerable to the positive and negative influences all around us, this early stage of development sets the foundation for who we are and who we will become.

No childhood is perfect. We all get into trouble, experience the mistakes of our parents, push boundaries, rebel. This trial-and-error learning results in both positive and negative consequences. Thankfully, as children we are resilient. When our needs are met more times than not, we learn to trust others. We can initiate and complete tasks on our own, modulate emotions, and develop and maintain healthy friendships. Subsequently, children in these environments develop a strong identity and sense of self. When caregivers do not meet needs on a consistent basis or the child experiences abuse, neglect, or bullying, development may manifest significantly different thoughts and behaviors that lead to difficulty trusting others, a lack of self-control, an inability to create healthy relationships. We may feel inferior and unsure of who we are and question if we have value. Most children develop somewhere in between and remain resilient. However, the foundation for how a child perceives themselves and how they view others is formed early. Those early experiences and the memories thereof, whether positive or negative, guide us throughout our entire lives.

This collection of photographs looks back at early childhood memories and externalizes a personal story in order to address both painful and joyful times, such is the process of psychotherapy. There is great value in looking back, in telling our story, and it takes courage to accept and then represent our personal truths in an honest way. Emotionally charged memories may bias our perspective as we recall only the positive and deny the negative; or we may focus on the negative, rejecting the positive and harboring bitterness, shame, anger, or sadness. This range of responses and feelings influences how we interact with our past, live our present, and consider our future.

There are many therapeutic ways to process our stories: journaling, talking to friends, engaging in creative endeavors, and participating in individual or group therapy. Processing our thoughts and feelings and being present with them, rather than avoiding them, allows us to come to terms with what can be modified and what cannot. These therapeutic measures allow us to identify the source of our feelings; decide how long to attend to the feelings; and determine if we want

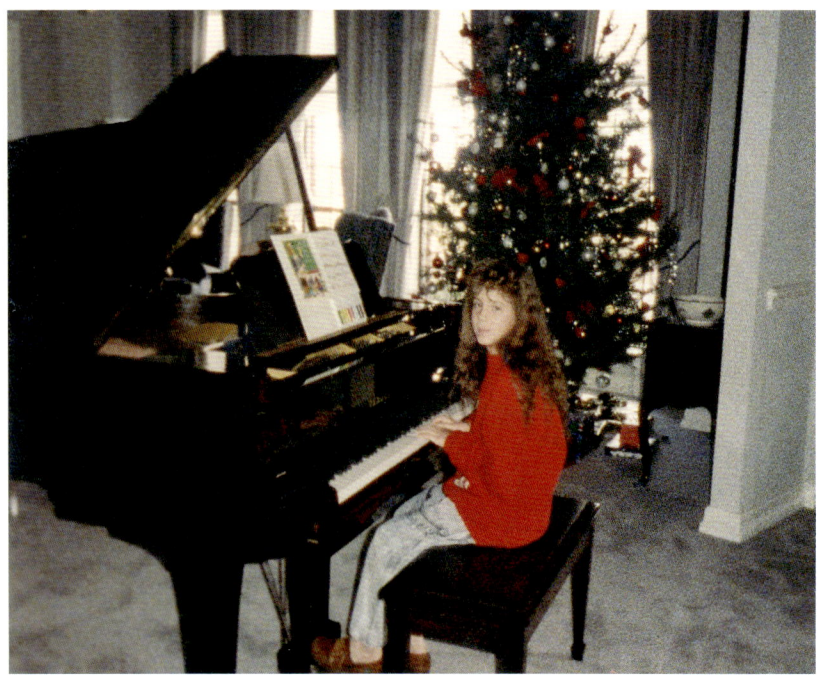

to continue to be influenced by those feelings whose origins are in the past. We then have the insight and ability to not allow past negative experiences to hinder our growth and block our progress in the present or future. From this process, we may accept an integration of our positive and negative experiences, developing a more realistic view of our self and a stronger sense of competence and confidence.

Once we move beyond past hurts and courageously integrate the whole of our experiences, the theme of our story may change. Emotional healing takes place. We can recall positive experiences and relationships we once had, even if imperfect. Confidence and insight to re-create what was helpful, valuable, and nurturing develops as, over time, we grow above our circumstances and release disappointments from childhood. We learn to pass on love, empathy, and compassion to the next generation. The full extent of this restorative process plays out in this collection of photographs that interprets an integrated whole of the photographer's life story, testifying to a range of truths to which we all, in turn, bear witness.

# THE DIFFICULT
# BUSINESS OF BEING HUMAN

by Diane Durant

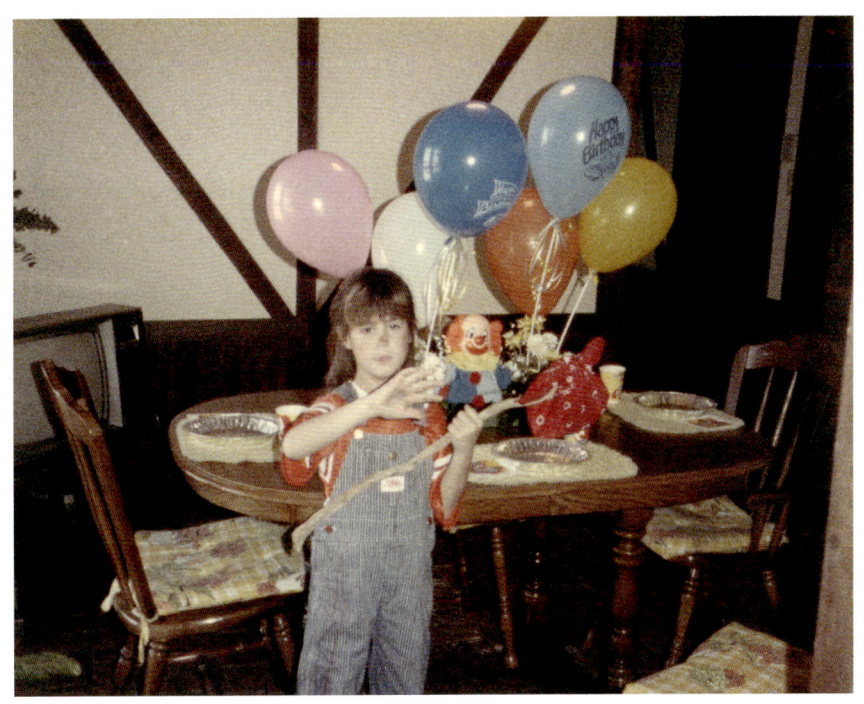

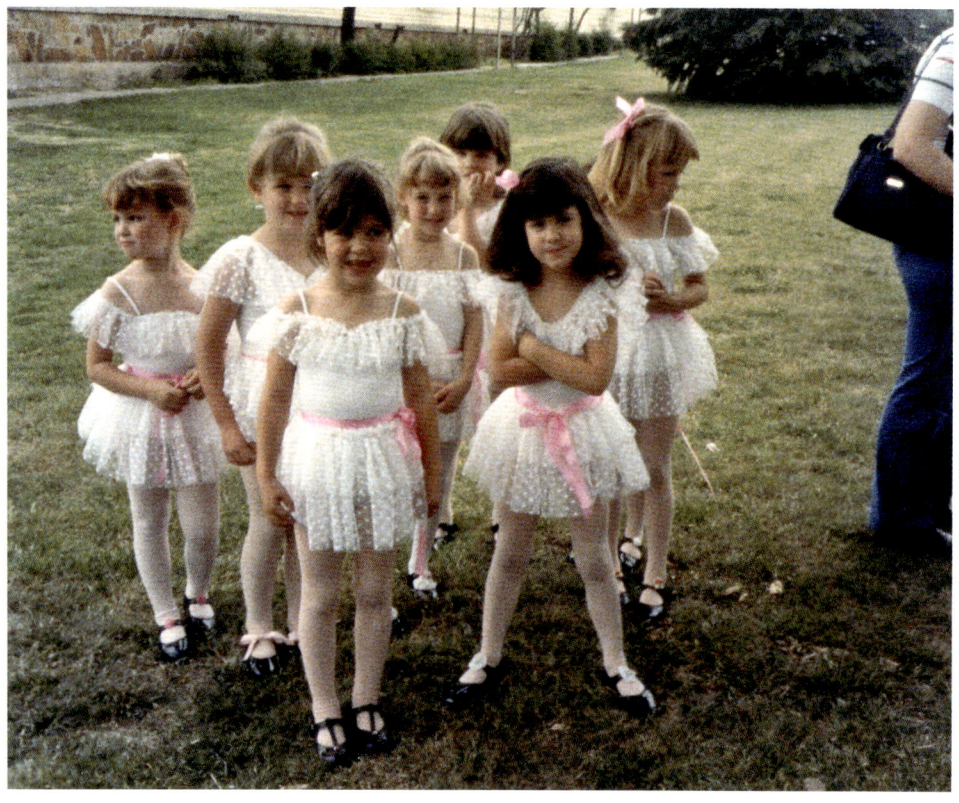

*everyone yelling?* I hid in the holly bushes (both literal and metaphorical) from 1986 to '88, squeezing my eyes tight so I couldn't see or hear or feel the chaos that may or may not have been as traumatic as I remember. But there are moments, flashes of reality burned into my psyche, woven into the person that I am and that I am continuously becoming—or maybe even *un*becoming—and these moments have shaped both my fictions and my truths. *Stories, 1986–88* is a little bit of both, a photographic reconciliation of all the things I couldn't change with all the things that never were, with a dash of adult-level cynicism and a handful of childlike innocence—a synergy as compelling as it is relatable, if not entertaining, hopefully.

Growing up isn't easy. We spend our whole childhood wishing it away, wishing we were older, wishing we could do the things our big brothers got to do, that we could ride our bikes to school even though we'd moved and would have to cross two highways now, there and back.

But our childhoods are only the beginning—obviously of our lives, but also of all the disappointment the world will divvy up and how we'll learn to deal with it, from something as innocuous as not getting to play the trumpet to the more painfully existential questions like, *Who am I? How'd I get here? Why is*

Years ago in graduate school, I remember reading an interview with French writer and conceptual artist Sophie Calle in which she confessed that in each of her works, her creative explorations, there was always a lie. Something she thought she would find but didn't. As an artist, an aspect of her process included giving herself something that didn't exist (though perhaps it should have) and giving that something the same amount of narrative weight as the rest of the elements in her stories. Perhaps not coincidentally, her artist's book, *True Stories*, relies on a similar pretense—and a consensual relationship between reader and narrator—as this book you're holding now. These are true stories, even if, to a degree, the contrarieties and juxtapositions are truths that I thought I would find but didn't, or truths that I knew existed but wanted to rewrite. Rephotograph. Reclaim.

When this restorative process began, first out of therapeutic necessity and then out of pure curiosity, I wasn't prepared to find—er, accept—some of my family's truths, mostly because I didn't know what to make of the bad times and I wasn't creatively concerned with the good times. Which, by the way, was also a tricked out Chevy van conversion complete with a 10" CRT color TV and built-in VCR that we road-tripped to Hobbs, New Mexico, for a basketball tournament in the summer of 1988, when adventure meant returning our Blockbuster rentals a week late and washing our uniforms with Woolite in the motel sink. Those were good times, indeed. And there were many. But the good times aren't what landed me in therapy twenty years later, pining after answers to the deeply philosophical questions of my youth and the very real traumas of the, well, bad times. And there were many.

I wasn't supposed to talk about the alcoholism and the anger, the fear or the confusion, and I'm probably still not. But those truths shaped me into the woman I am today, into the mother I am definitely, just as much as my proclivities for arcade games and the art of sarcasm that seem more biological than environmental. But parsing out the nature versus nurture debate in real time was more than my adolescence could bear, and so I waited, mostly until I could trust myself to handle all possible outcomes, to make proverbial lemonade out of life's lemons, to rephotograph a carefree childhood that was anything but. So here we are. Of course, I've not set out on this trek alone, and I have my friends, family, colleagues, therapist, and you to thank for helping me turn these stories into reality, even if that reality is what I had hoped to find but didn't.

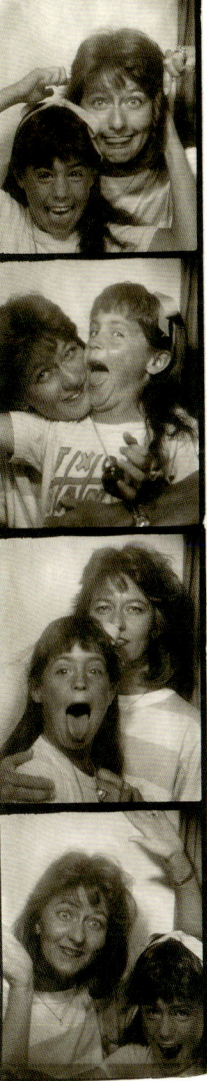
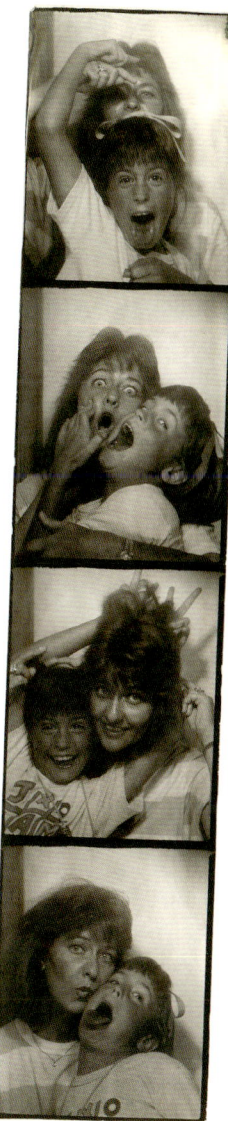

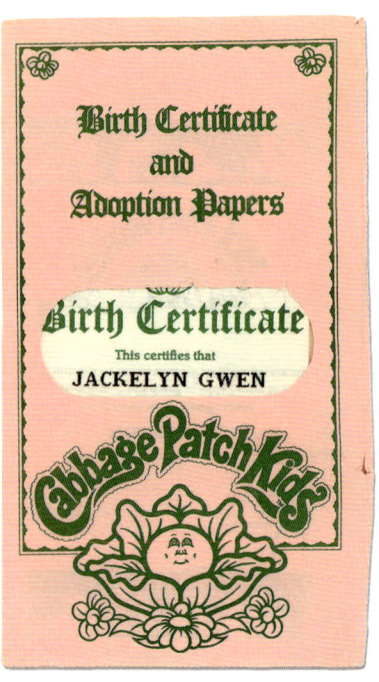

**Birth Certificate and Adoption Papers**

**Birth Certificate**

This certifies that

**JACKELYN GWEN**

Cabbage Patch Kids

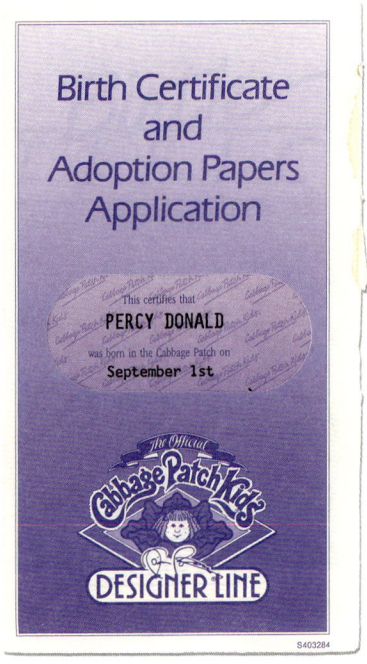

**Birth Certificate and Adoption Papers Application**

This certifies that

**PERCY DONALD**

was born in the Cabbage Patch on

**September 1st**

The Official Cabbage Patch Kids

**DESIGNER LINE**

S403284

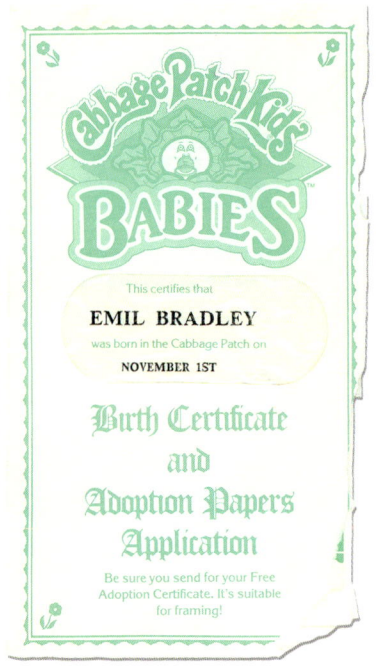

**Cabbage Patch Kids BABIES**

This certifies that

**EMIL BRADLEY**

was born in the Cabbage Patch on

**NOVEMBER 1ST**

**Birth Certificate and Adoption Papers Application**

Be sure you send for your Free Adoption Certificate. It's suitable for framing!

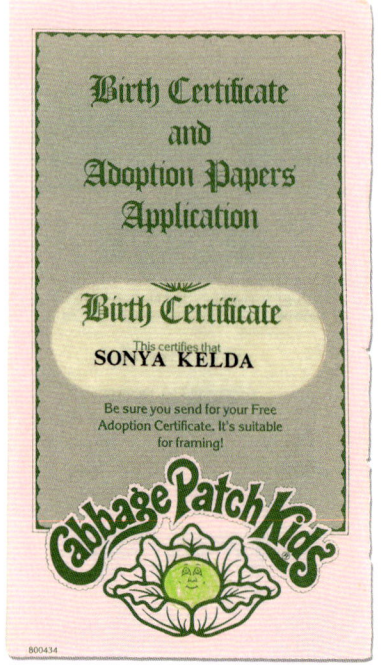

**Birth Certificate and Adoption Papers Application**

**Birth Certificate**

This certifies that

**SONYA KELDA**

Be sure you send for your Free Adoption Certificate. It's suitable for framing!

Cabbage Patch Kids

800434

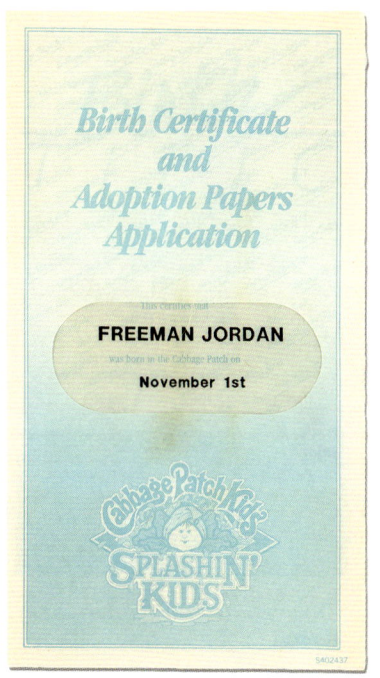

*Birth Certificate
and
Adoption Papers
Application*

This certifies that

**FREEMAN JORDAN**

was born in the Cabbage Patch on

**November 1st**

Cabbage Patch Kids
SPLASHIN' KIDS

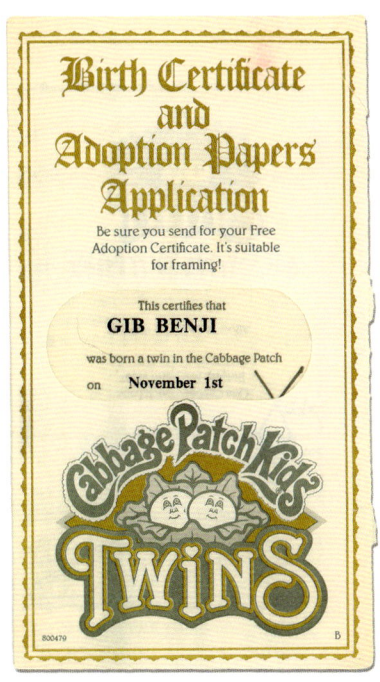

# Birth Certificate and Adoption Papers Application

Be sure you send for your Free
Adoption Certificate. It's suitable
for framing!

This certifies that

**GIB BENJI**

was born a twin in the Cabbage Patch

on **November 1st**

Cabbage Patch Kids
TWINS

800479                                    B

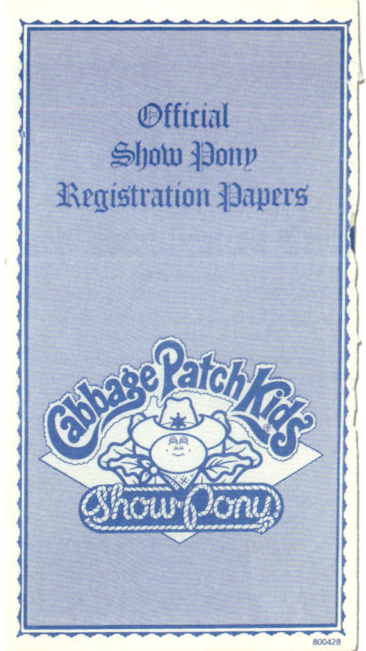

*Official
Show Pony
Registration Papers*

Cabbage Patch Kids
Show Pony

800428

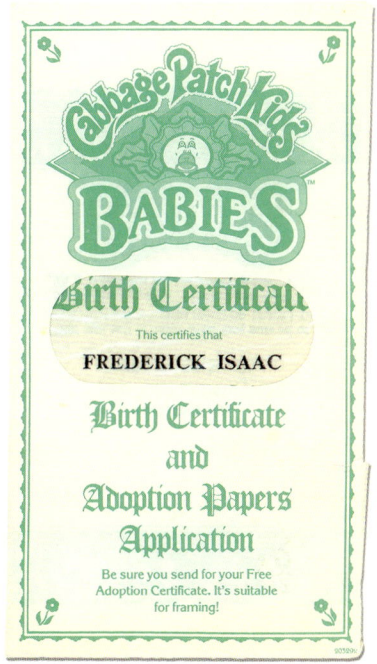

# Cabbage Patch Kids
## BABIES

### Birth Certificate

This certifies that

**FREDERICK ISAAC**

Birth Certificate
and
Adoption Papers
Application

Be sure you send for your Free
Adoption Certificate. It's suitable
for framing!

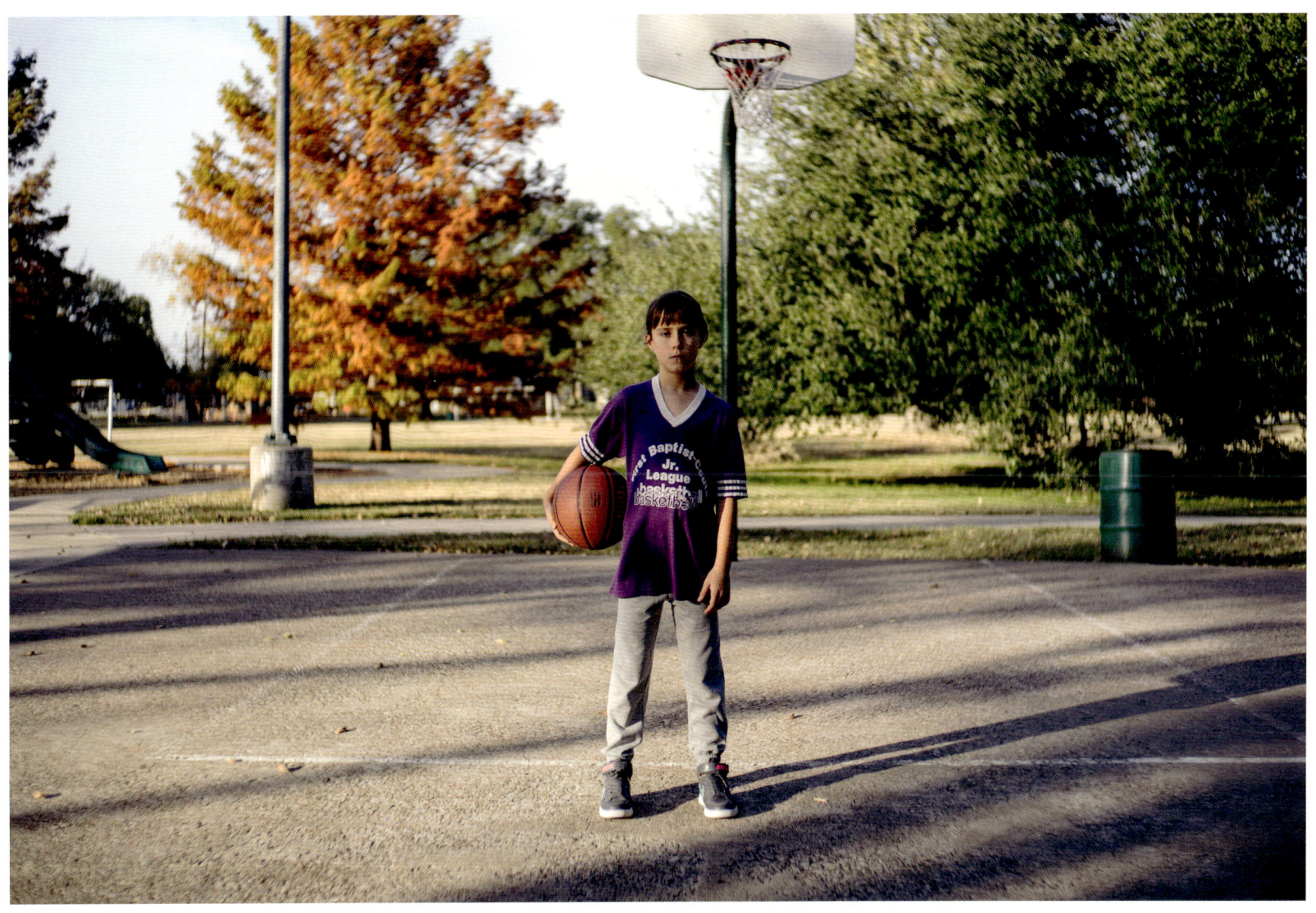

MY FRIEND CAROL AUTOMATICALLY HYPERVENTILATED EVERY TIME SHE LOST THE BALL. I AUTOMATICALLY MISSED EVERY ENSUING LAYUP. BECAUSE THAT'S WHAT FRIENDS ARE FOR.

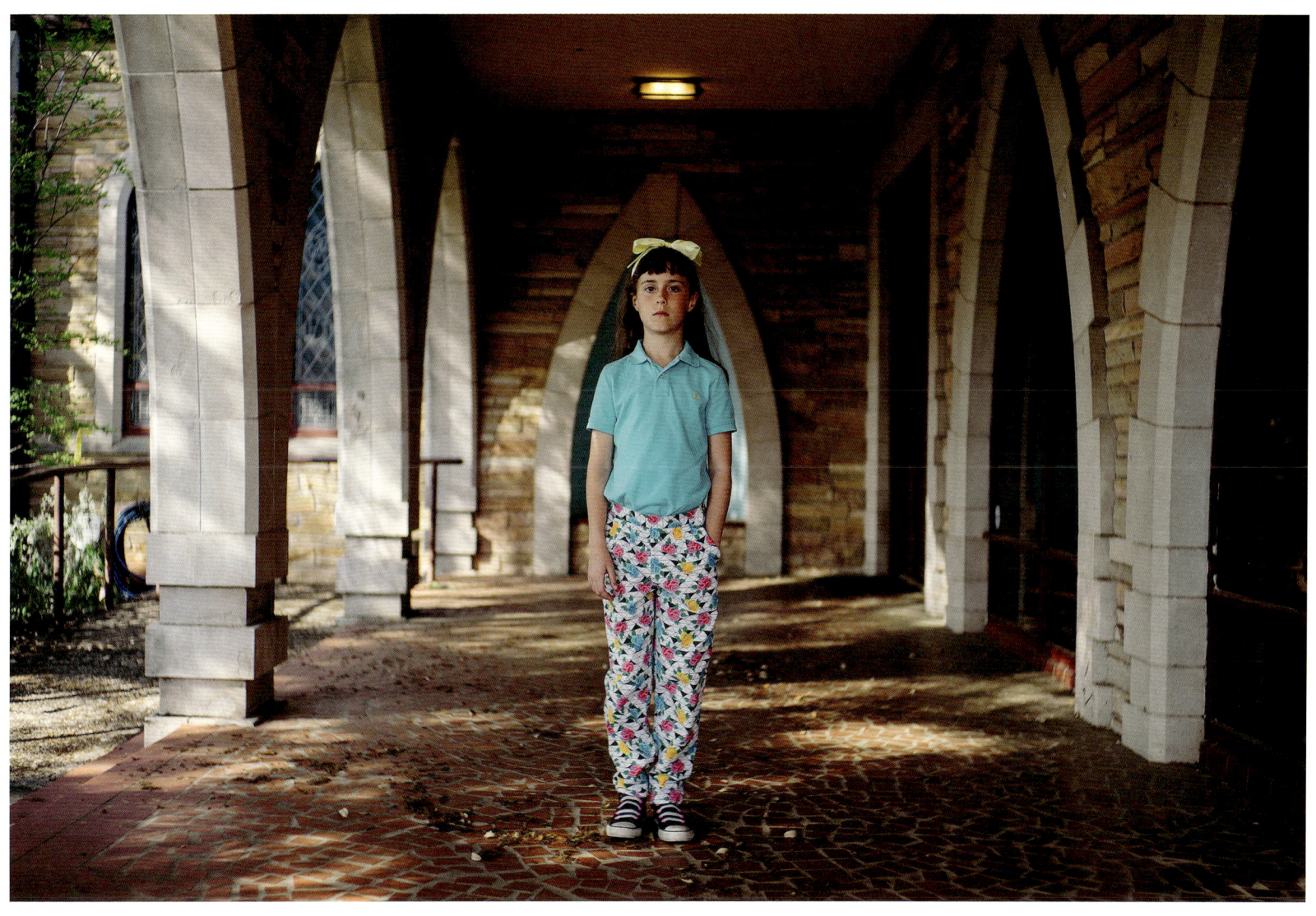

I WOKE UP EARLY EVERY SUNDAY MORNING TO PRAY TO GOD THAT I DIDN'T HAVE TO PUT ON A DRESS AND GO TO CHURCH. I'LL NEVER FORGET THE DAY HE FINALLY ANSWERED.

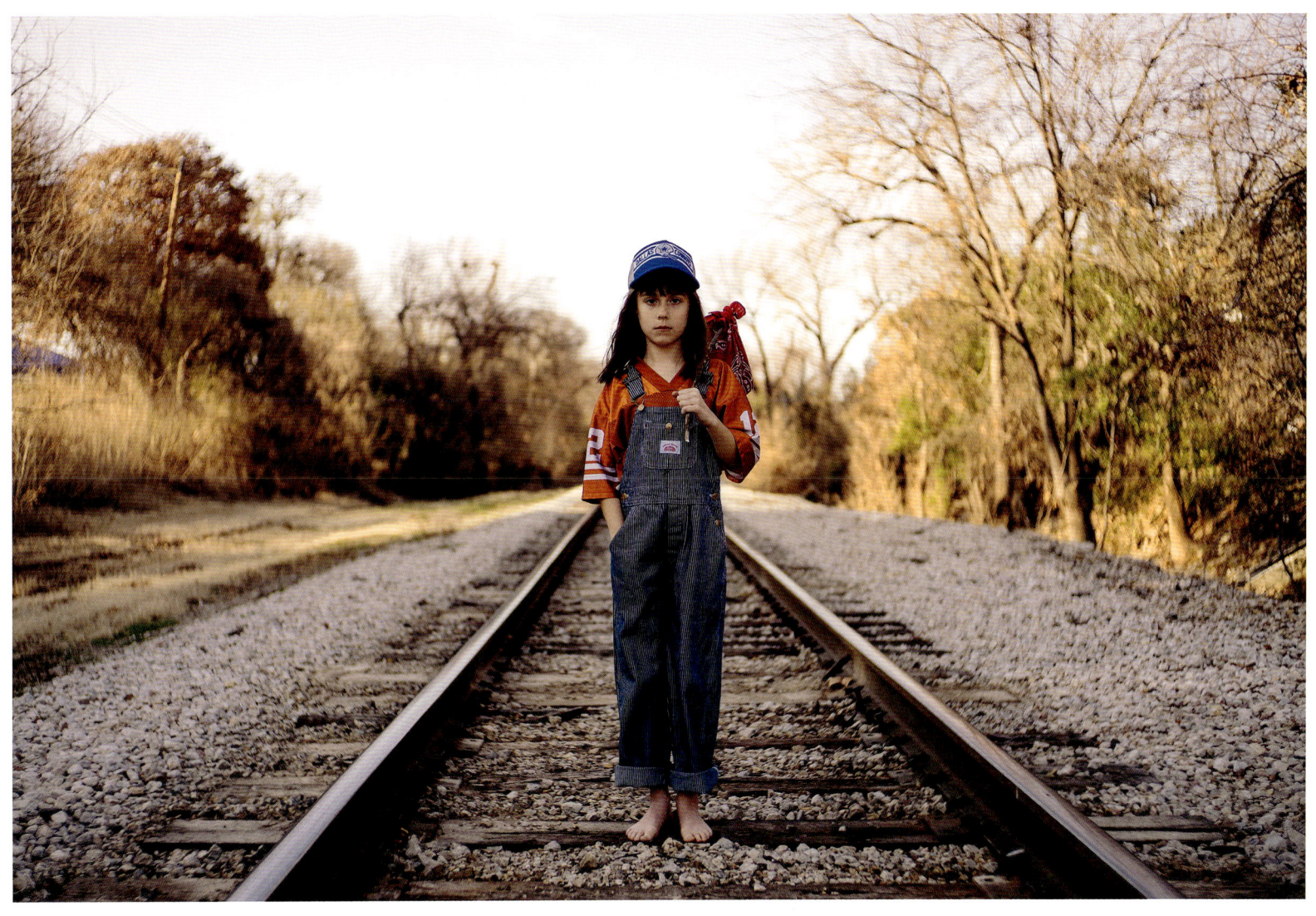

THE CLOSEST I EVER CAME TO THE TRANSIENT LIFE OF MY DREAMS WAS A HOBO-THEMED
BIRTHDAY PARTY. COME AS YOU ARE, THE INVITATIONS SAID,
WHICH WAS ALL I NEEDED TO HEAR.

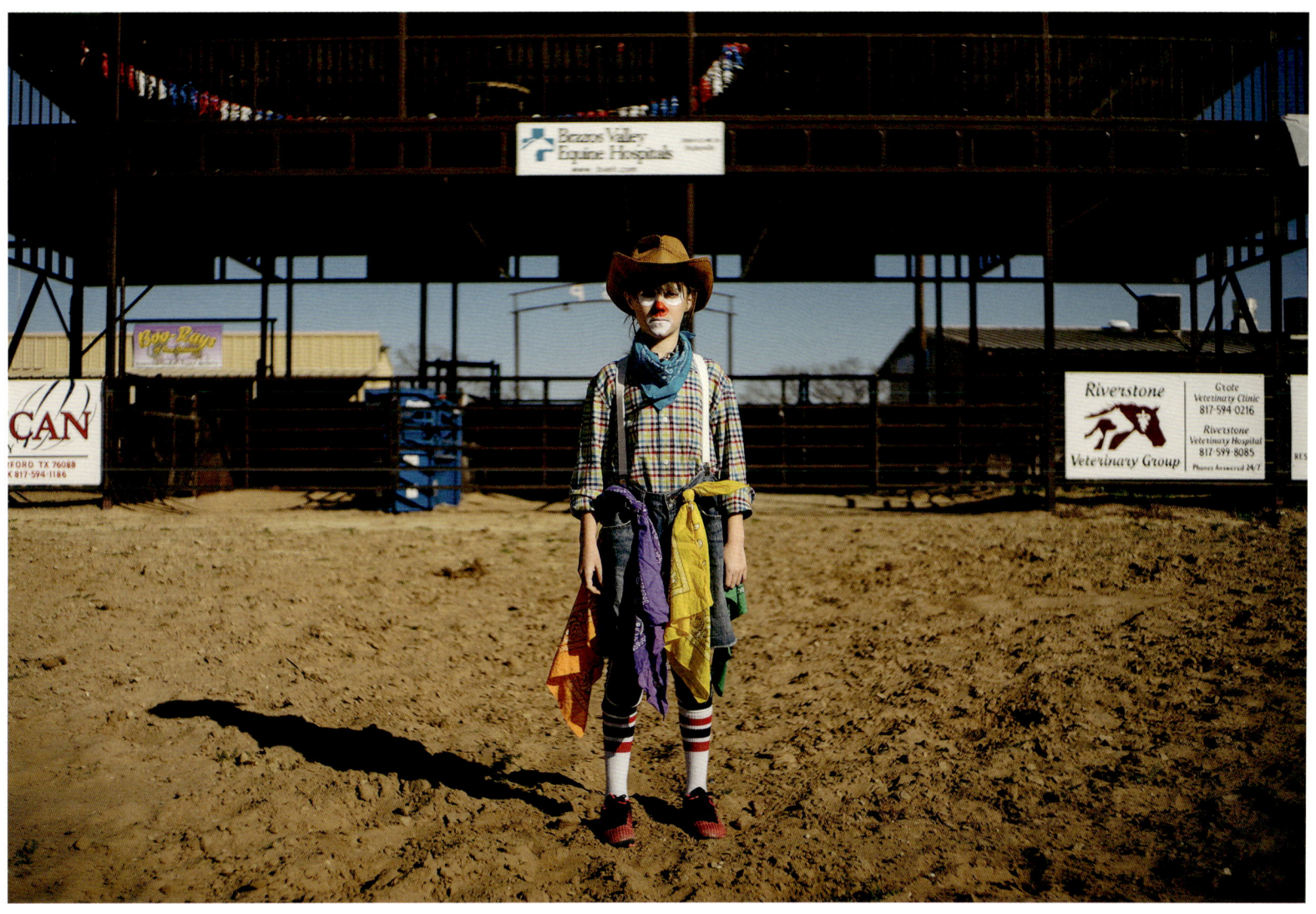

"YOU COULD BE THE SHERIFF'S POSSE SWEETHEART ONE DAY," THEY WOULD SAY.
BUT THAT WASN'T THE BEST PART OF THE RODEO.

THIRTEEN TIMES I WAS A FLOWER GIRL, AND LIKE A
WEED, I LEARNED TO GROW WHERE I WAS PLANTED.

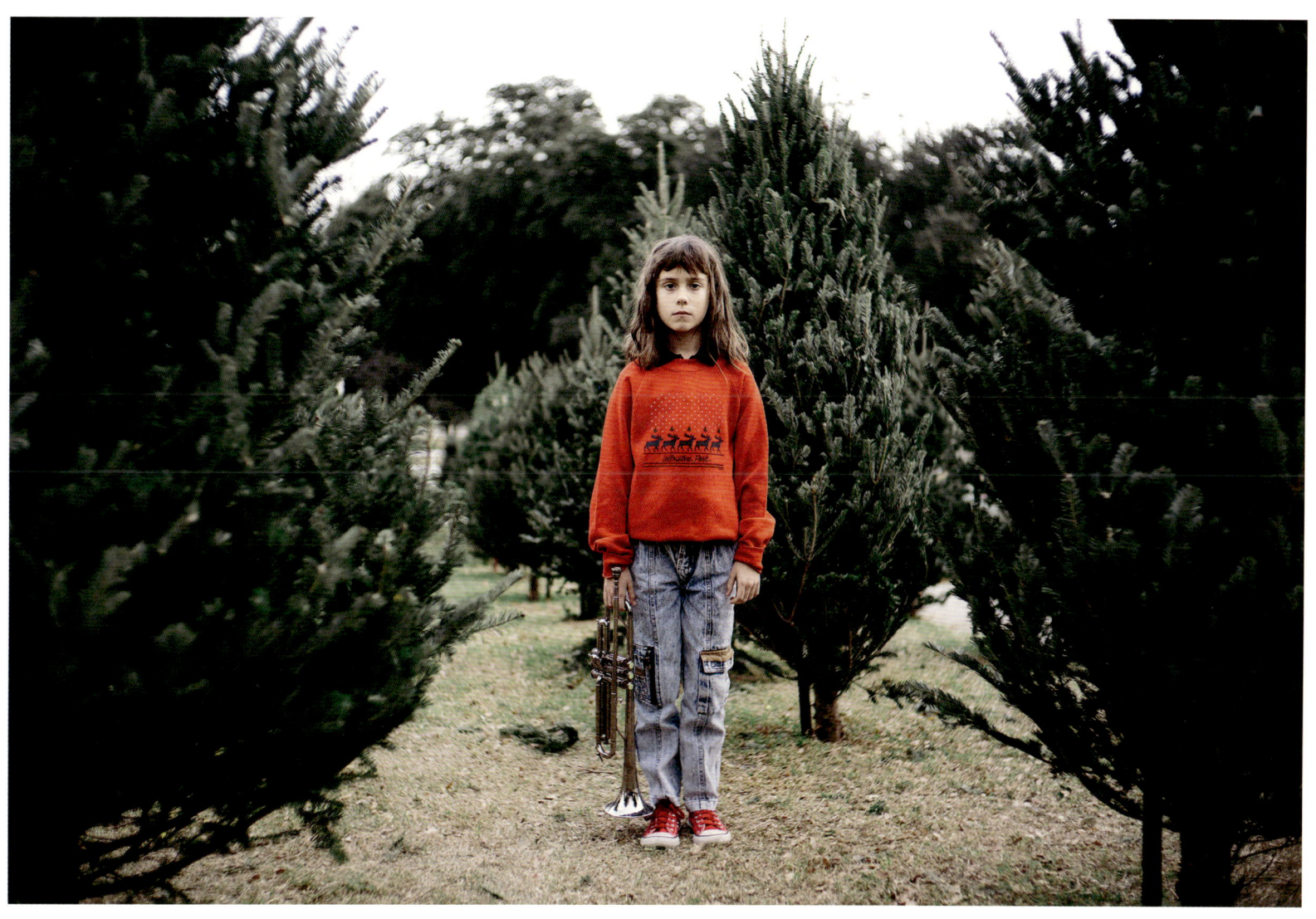

I PLAYED "THE TOYMAKER'S DANCE" AT MY WINTER PIANO RECITAL.
WHAT I REALLY WANTED TO PLAY WAS THE TRUMPET.

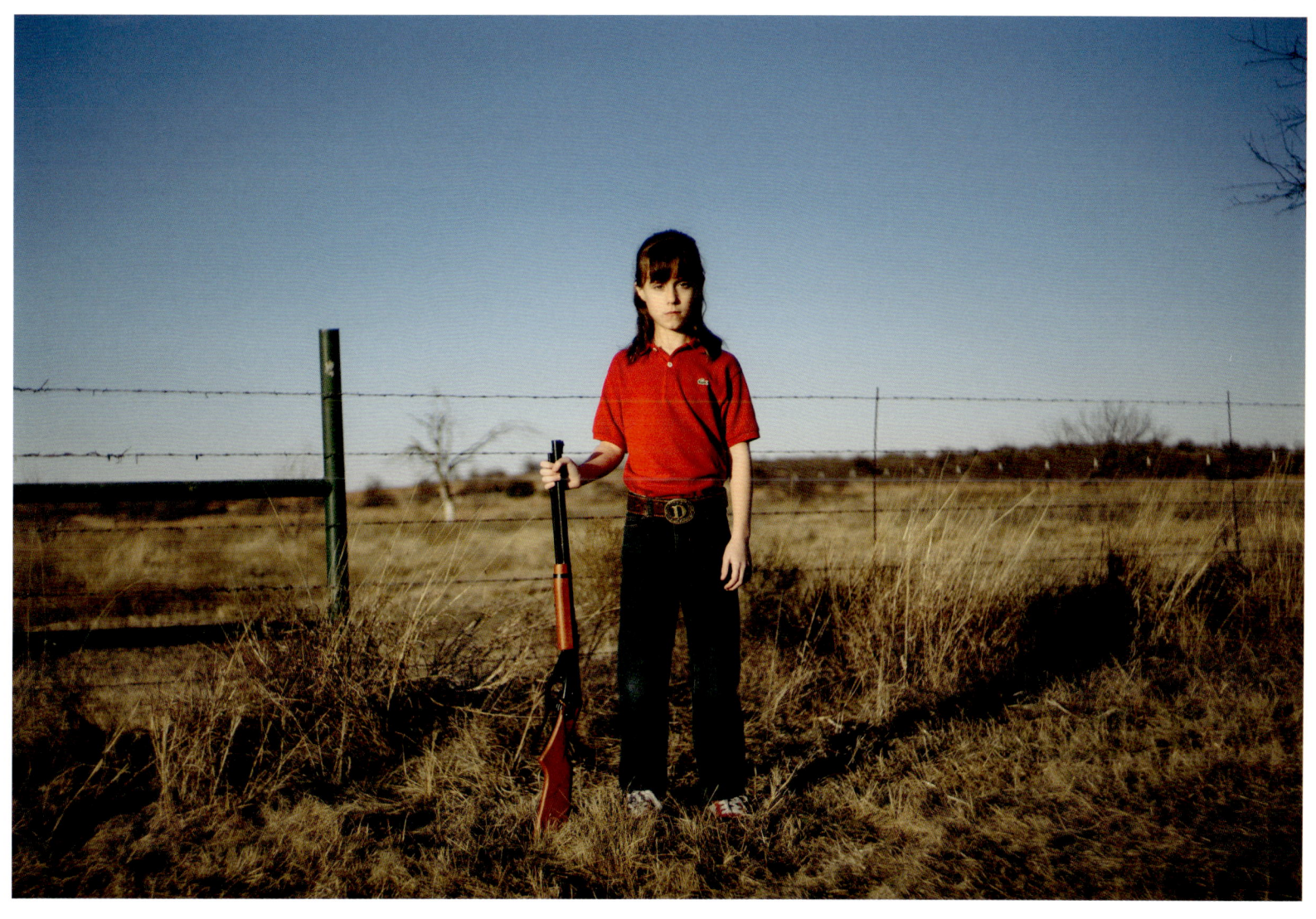

COKE CANS, TREE TRUNKS, PLASTIC BOTTLES, CLAY PIGEONS—I WAS ALWAYS THE BETTER
SHOT. TWENTY-THREE YEARS LATER, WITH A GUN TO HIS OWN HEAD,
MY BROTHER WOULD MISS AGAIN, THANK GOODNESS.

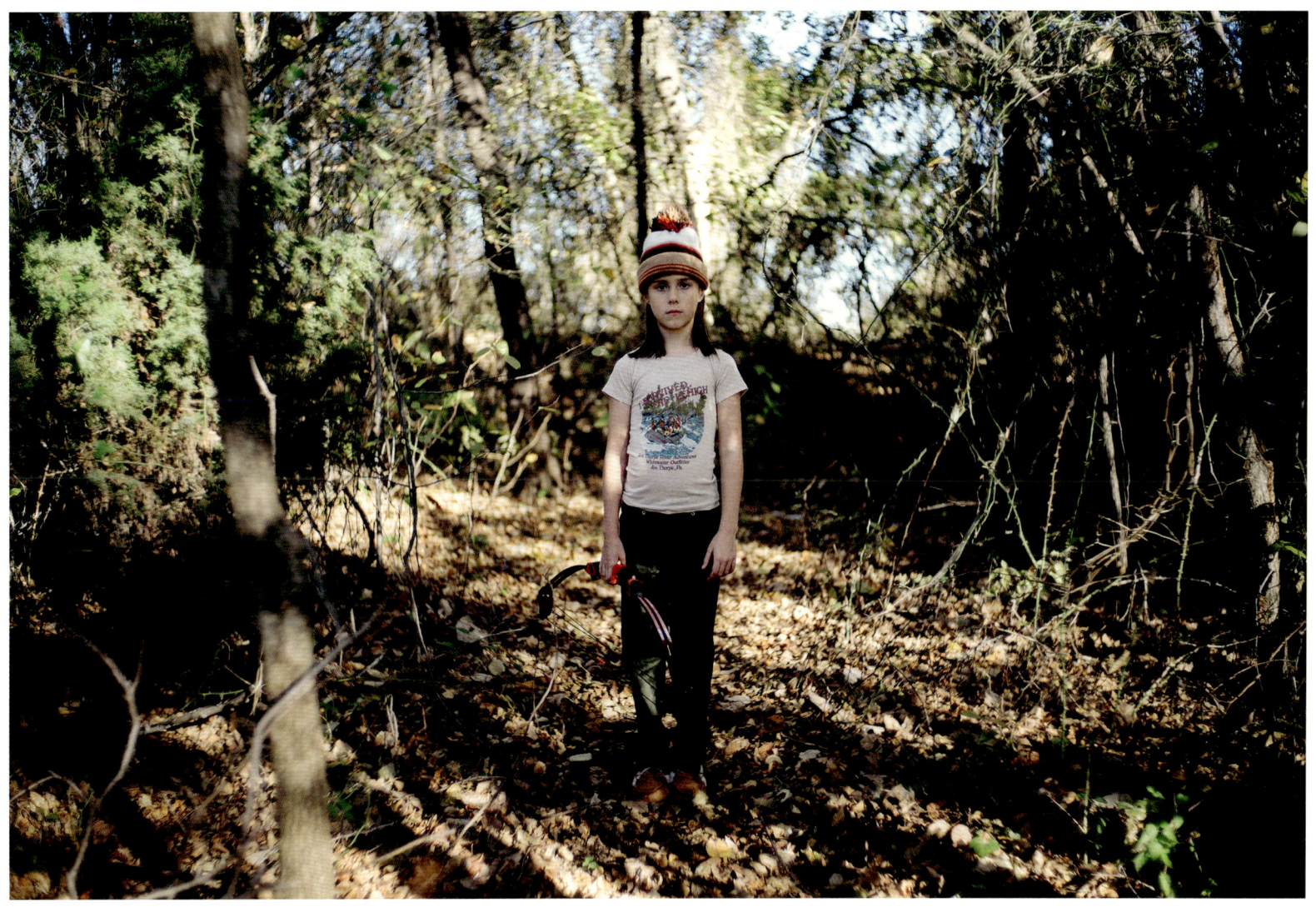

"MY LITTLE TOMBOY," SHE WOULD SAY, ALMOST APOLOGETICALLY. I
ONLY UNDERSTOOD THAT TO MEAN I COULDN'T WEAR CAMO AND
SHORT HAIR LIKE THE OTHER BOYS.

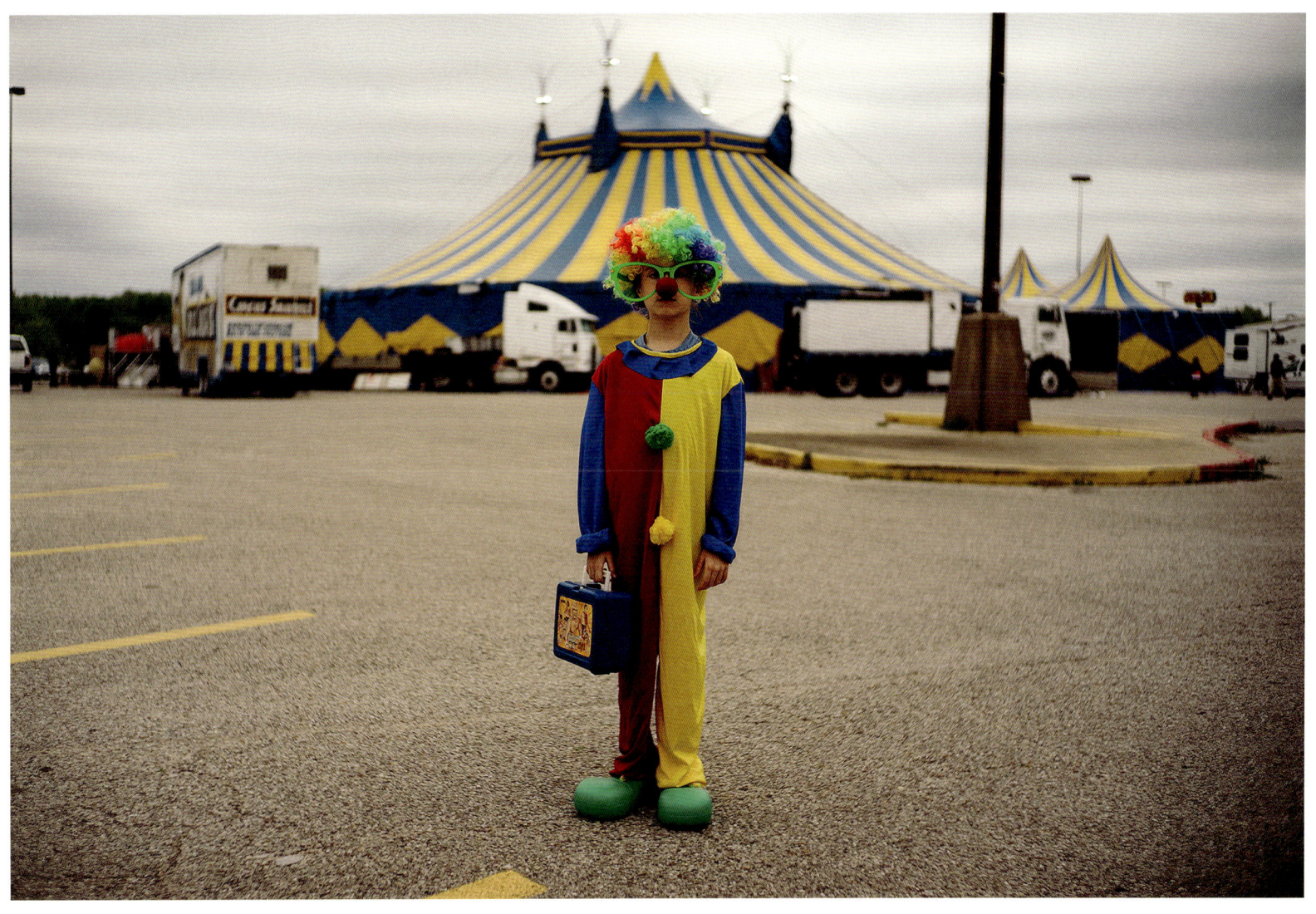

"ARE YOU GOING TO RUN AWAY AND JOIN THE CIRCUS?" THEY WOULD KID.
BUT CLOWN COLLEGE WAS NO JOKE.

THE GARDEN SNAIL CAN REACH SPEEDS UP TO .03 MILES AN HOUR.

I RAN LIKE THE WIND.

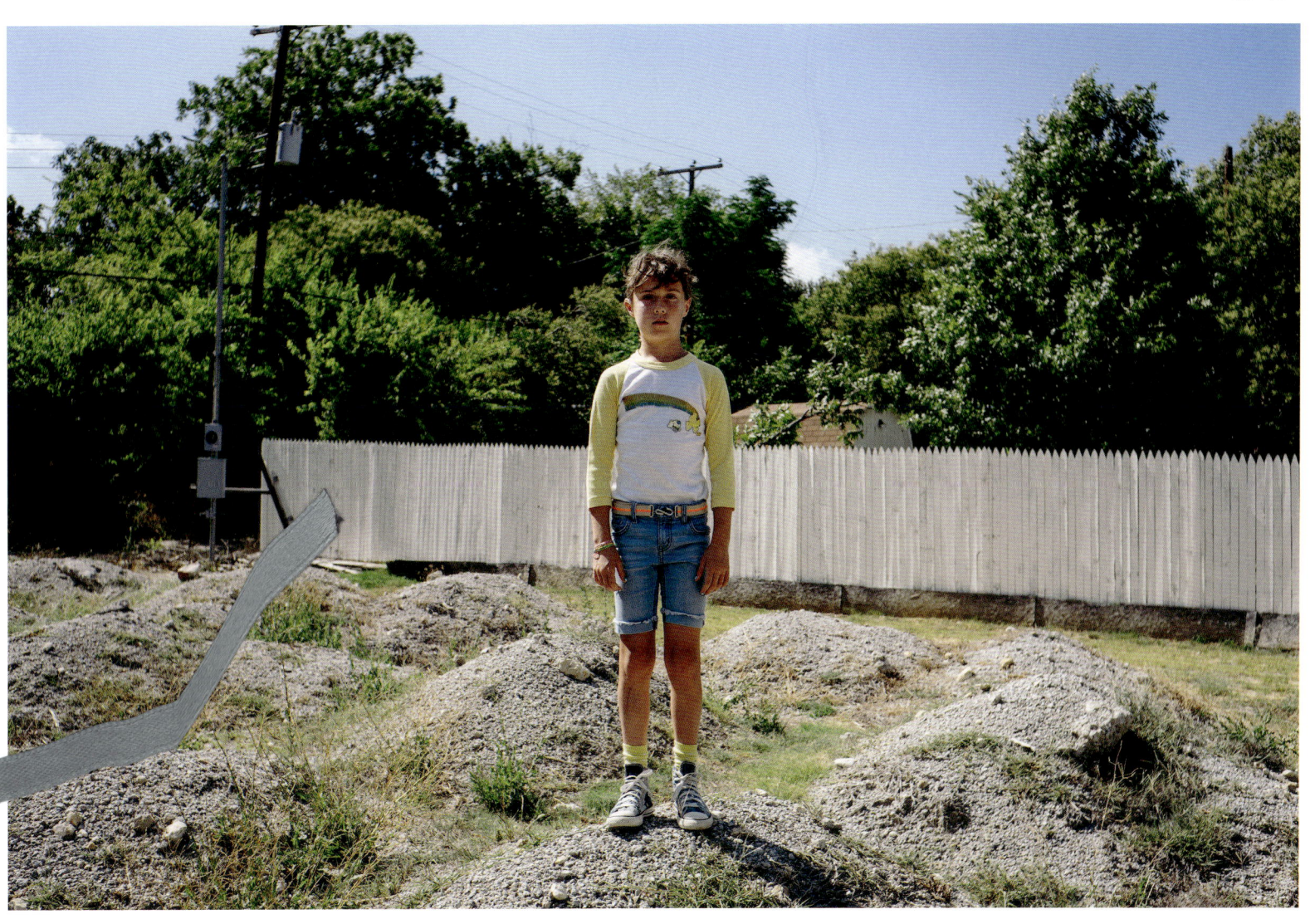

June 1986

THE VACANT LOT ACROSS THE STREET FROM OUR HOUSE WAS CALLED
THE JUMPS, AND IT ONLY HAD ONE RULE: BE HOME BY DINNER.

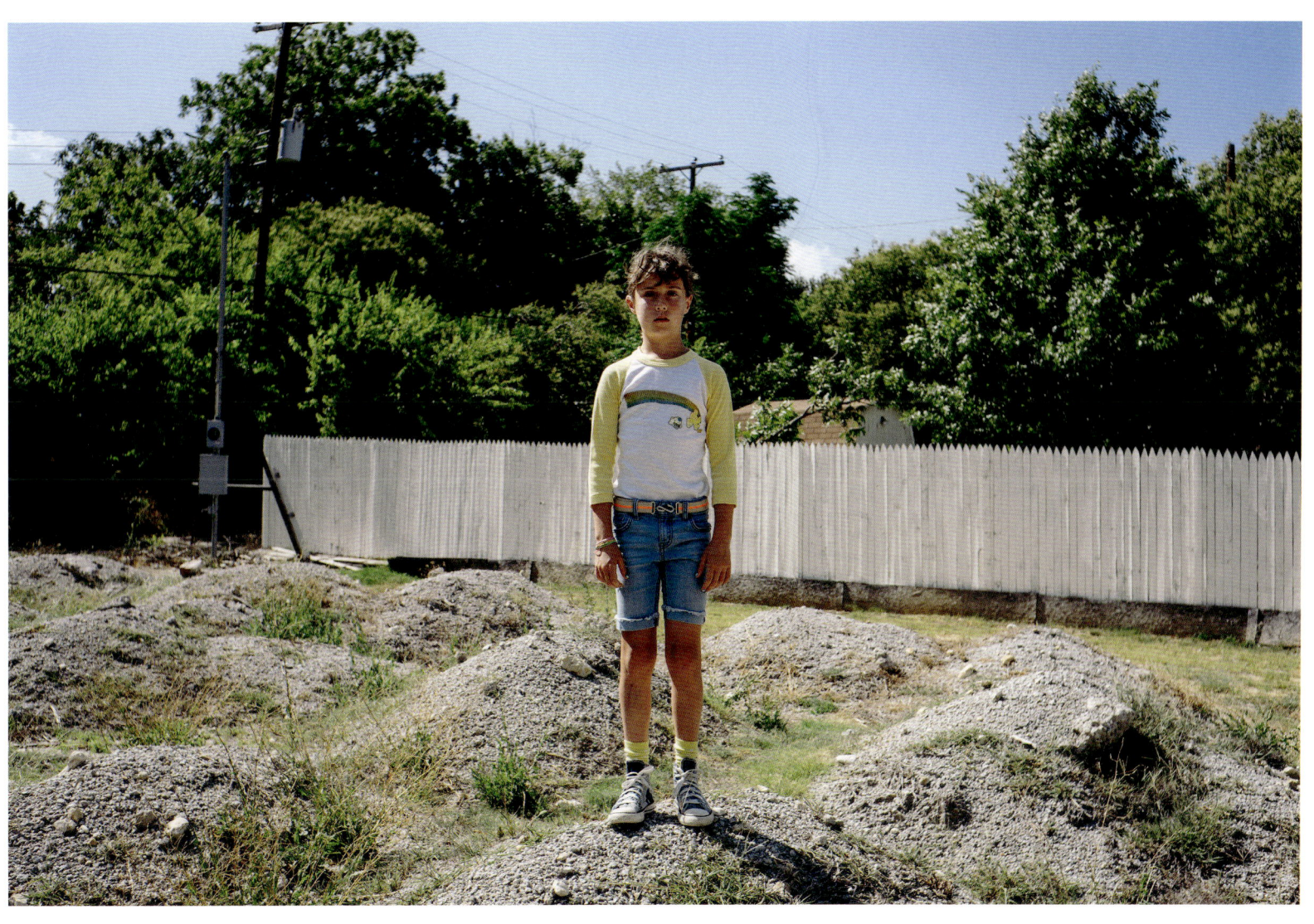

THE VACANT LOT ACROSS THE STREET FROM OUR HOUSE WAS CALLED
THE JUMPS, AND IT ONLY HAD ONE RULE: BE HOME BY DINNER.

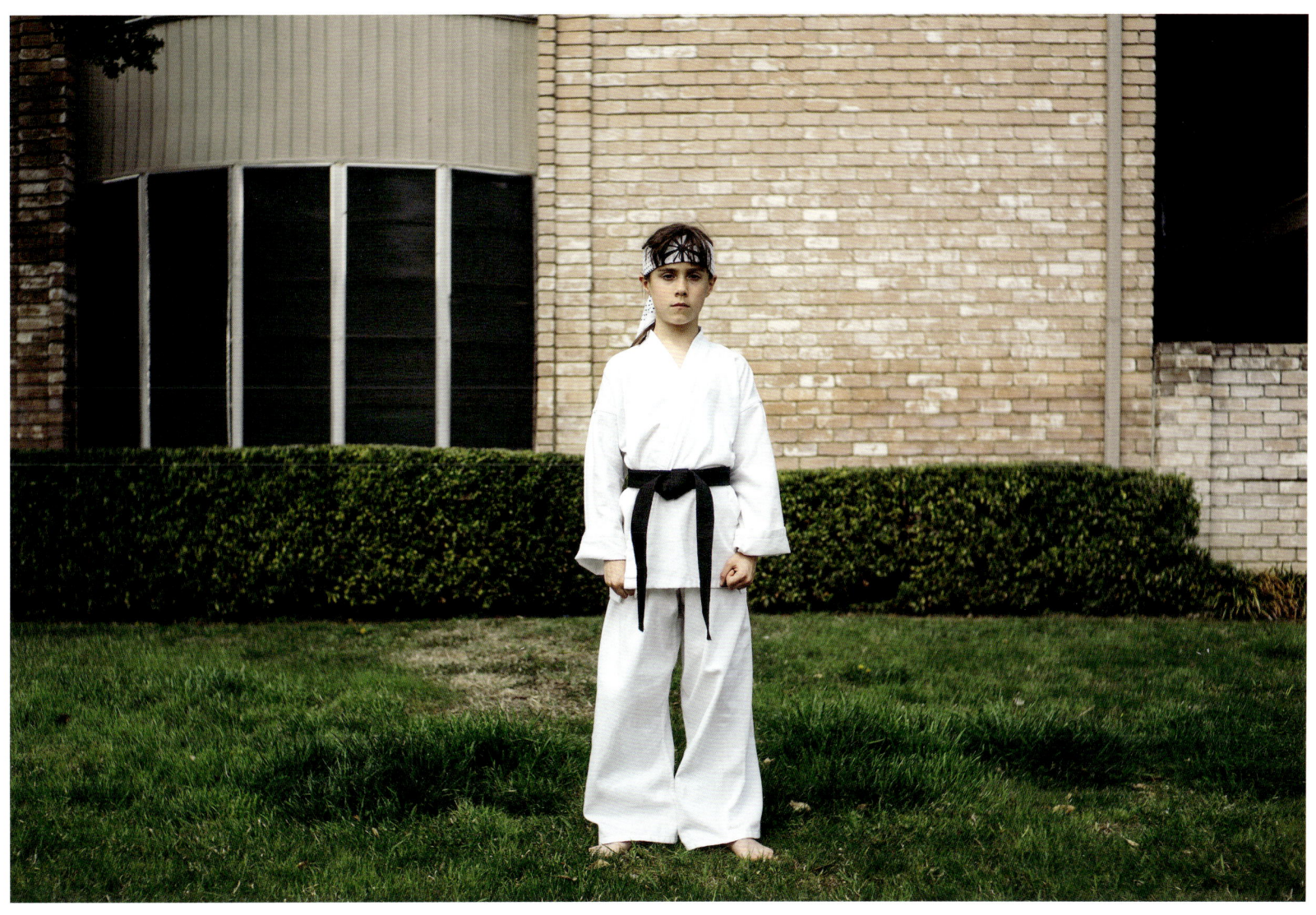

MY SECRET HIDING PLACE WAS IN THE HOLLY BUSHES OUTSIDE MY BEDROOM WINDOW.
I KEPT MY MOST TREASURED POSESSIONS SAFE THERE IN A HULK HOGAN LUNCHBOX.
DANNY LARUSSO WOULD TEACH ME EVERYTHING ELSE I NEEDED TO KNOW.

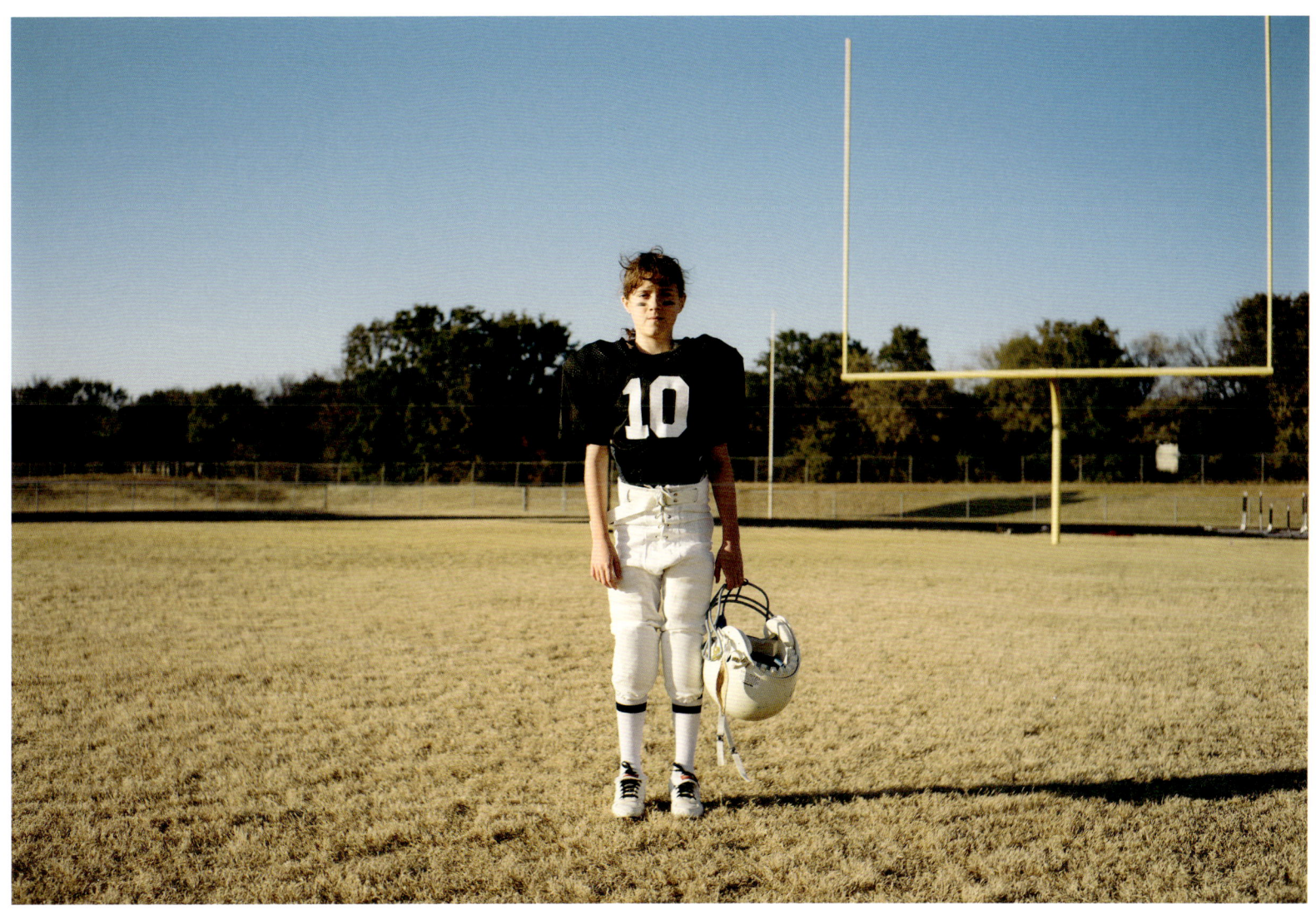

IF I COULD REWRITE THE LITTLE DITTY 'BOUT JACK AND DIANE, I'D BE THE FOOTBALL STAR.

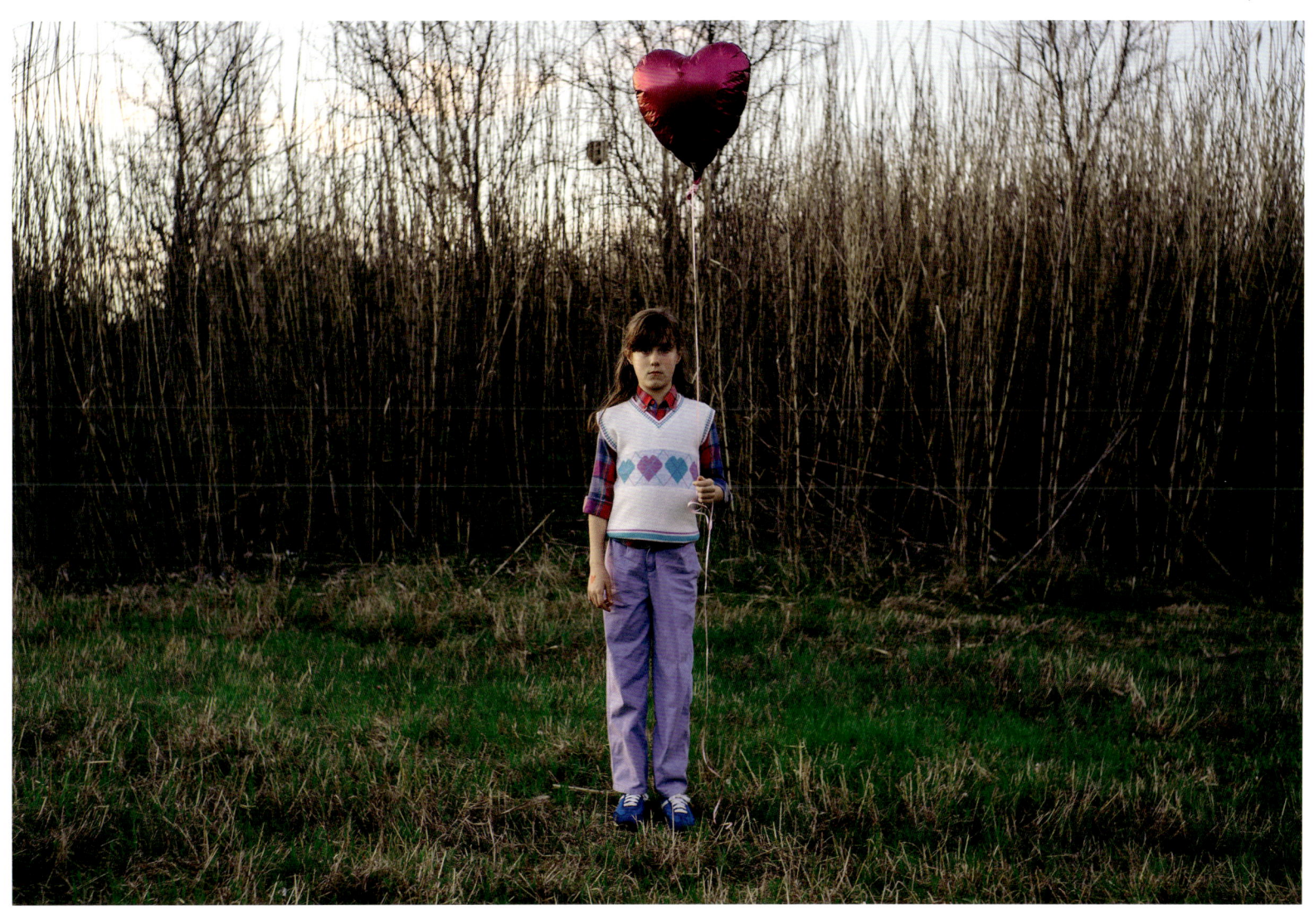

I WANTED TO KNOW WHAT LOVE WAS.
I WANTED SOMEONE TO SHOW ME.

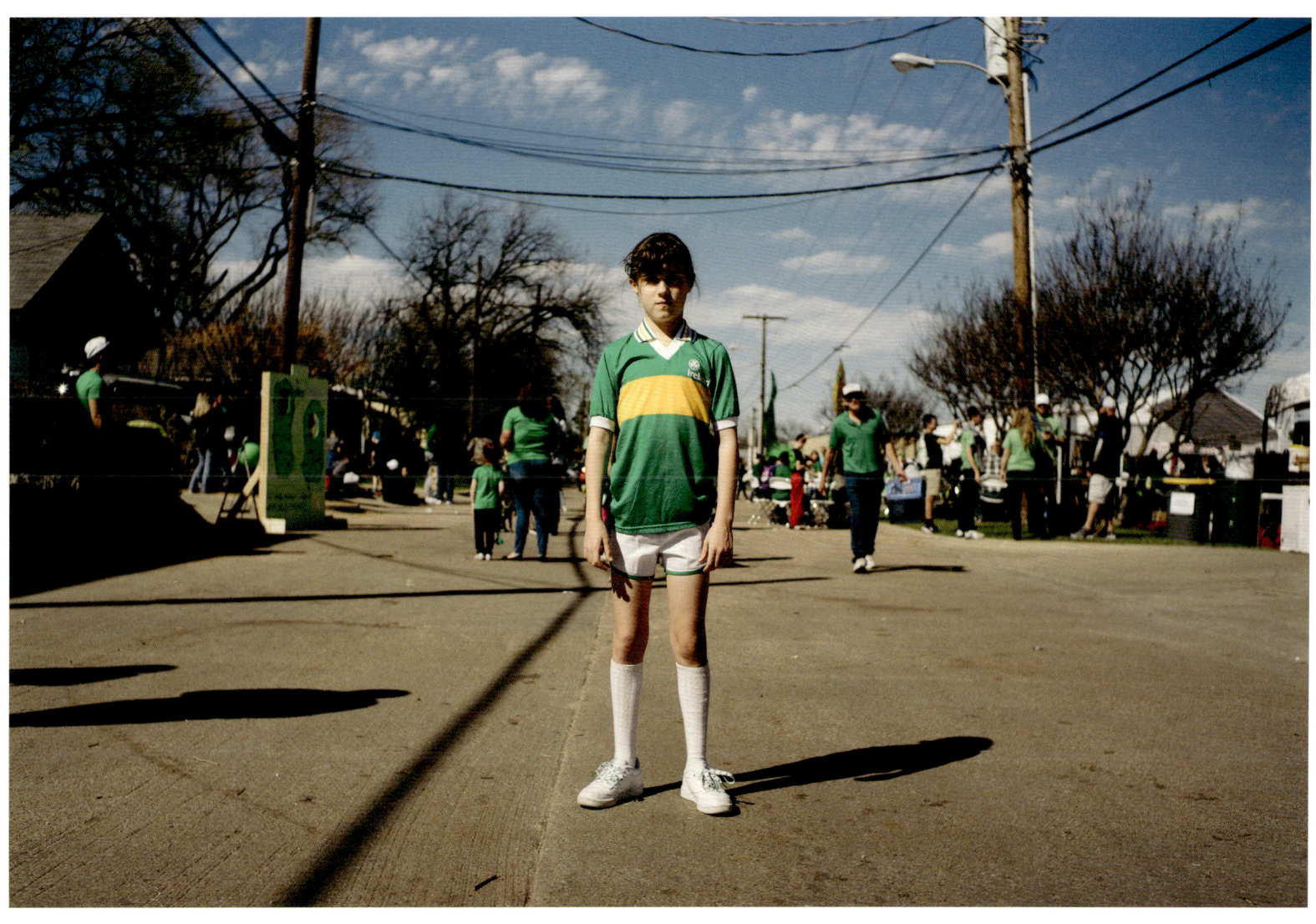

IN MY HEART, I ALWAYS KNEW I WAS IRISH, BUT IT WOULD BE THIRTY MORE YEARS
UNTIL I'D FIND MY PEOPLE. MY CLANN, AS IT WERE.

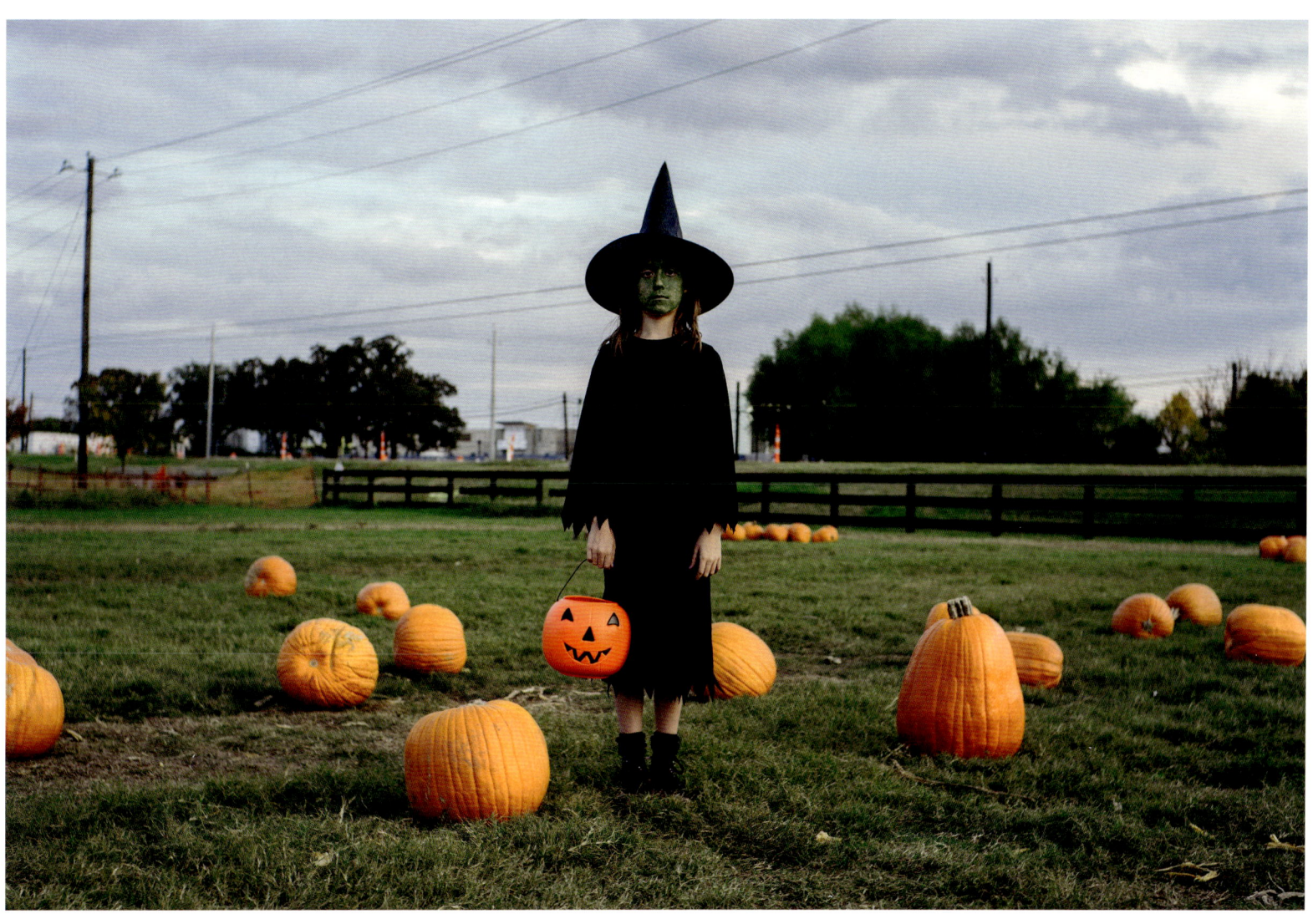

I WASN'T A CLOWN FOR HALLOWEEN, BECAUSE HALLOWEEN WAS FOR MAKE-BELIEVE.

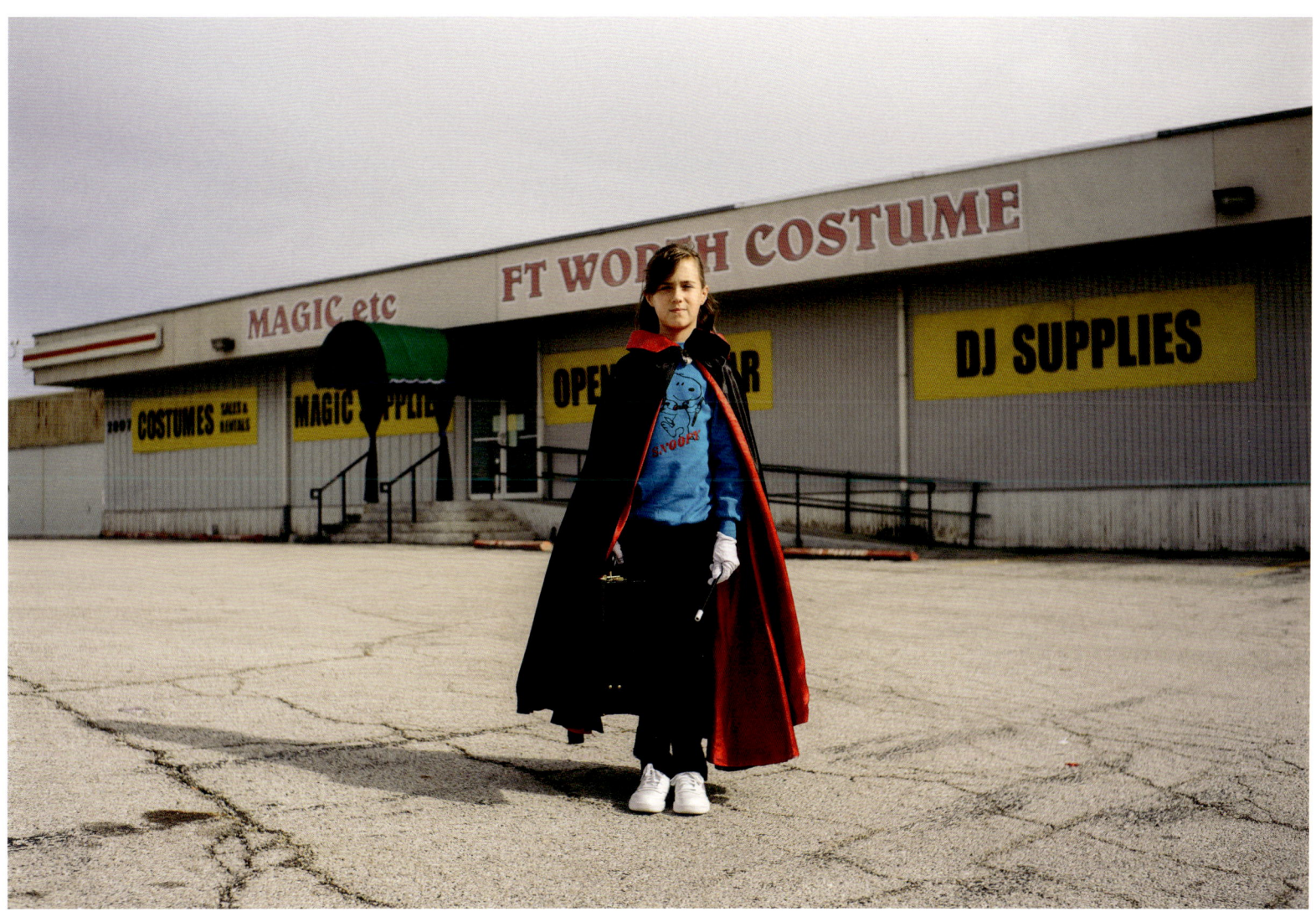

I THOUGHT ABOUT TRYING TO MAKE MYSELF DISAPPEAR,
BUT DEEP DOWN, I ONLY WANTED TO BE SEEN.

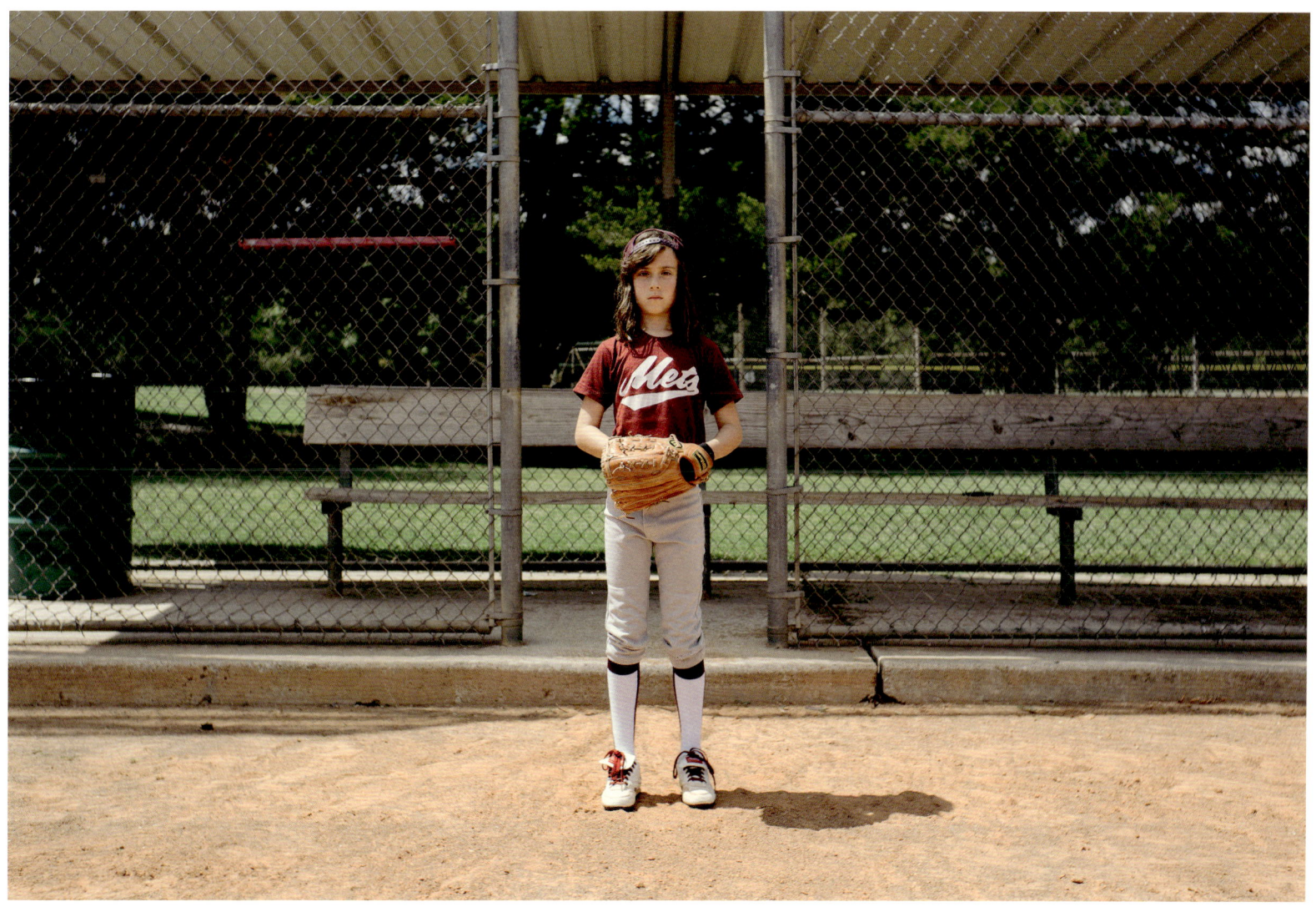

AS THE ONLY GIRL ON THE TEAM, I WASN'T THE STRONGEST PLAYER. OR THE FASTEST.
OR THE TOUGHEST. BUT I COULD LAY DOWN AN IMPOSSIBLE BUNT,
BECAUSE I WAS THE SMARTEST.

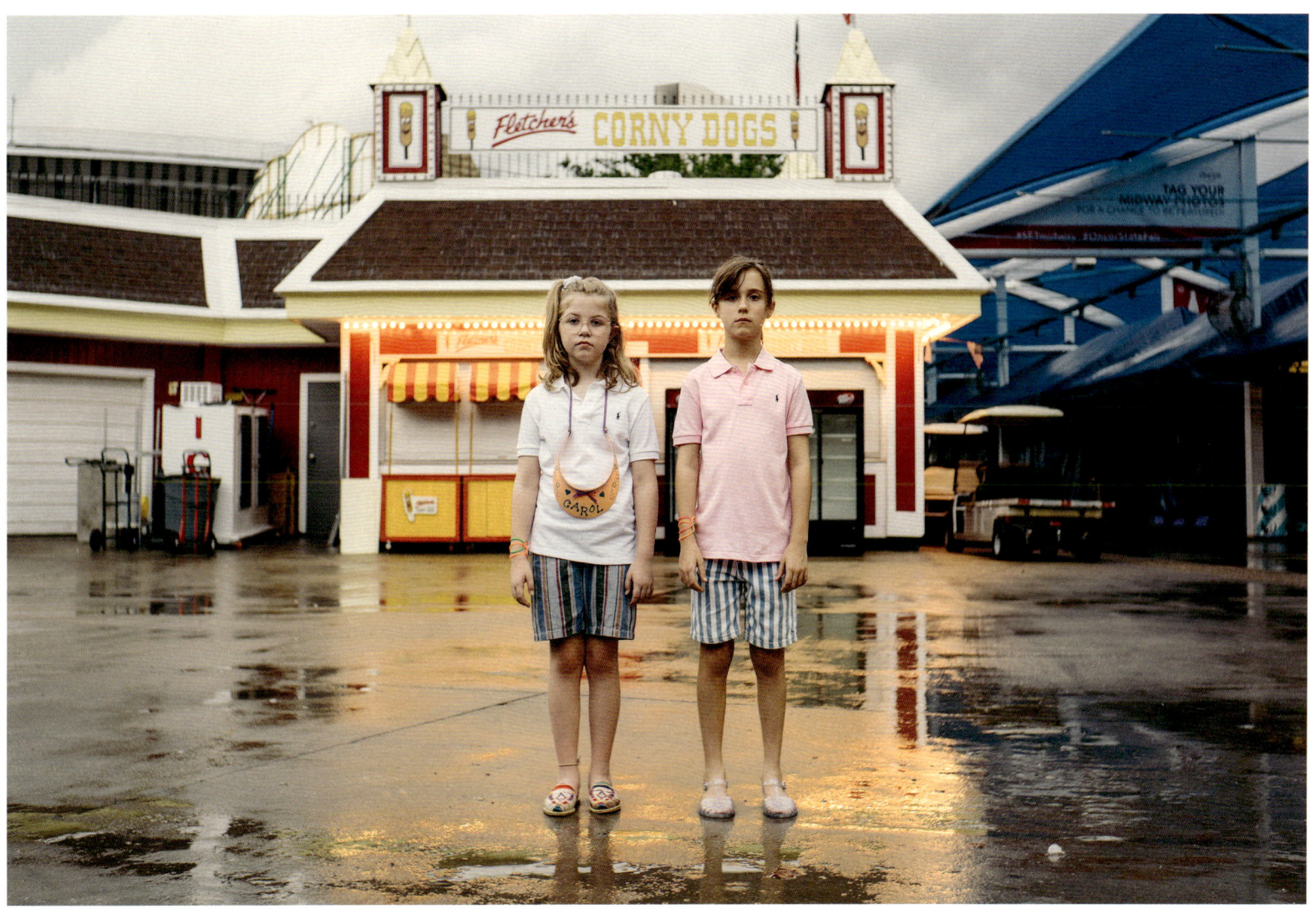

IF YOU DON'T LIKE THE WEATHER IN TEXAS, YOU'RE SUPPOSED TO WAIT FIVE MINUTES. THE WEATHER PROBABLY CHANGED 12 TIMES WHILE WE WAITED FOR A CORNY DOG, BUT IT WAS WORTH IT, ONCE A YEAR.

I CREDITED ALL ACCIDENTS AND MOST MISTAKES TO FRIEND, MY IMAGINARY FRIEND. WHEN WE MOVED IN 1987, FRIEND STAYED BEHIND, AND FROM THAT POINT FORWARD, I HAD NO ONE TO BLAME BUT MYSELF.

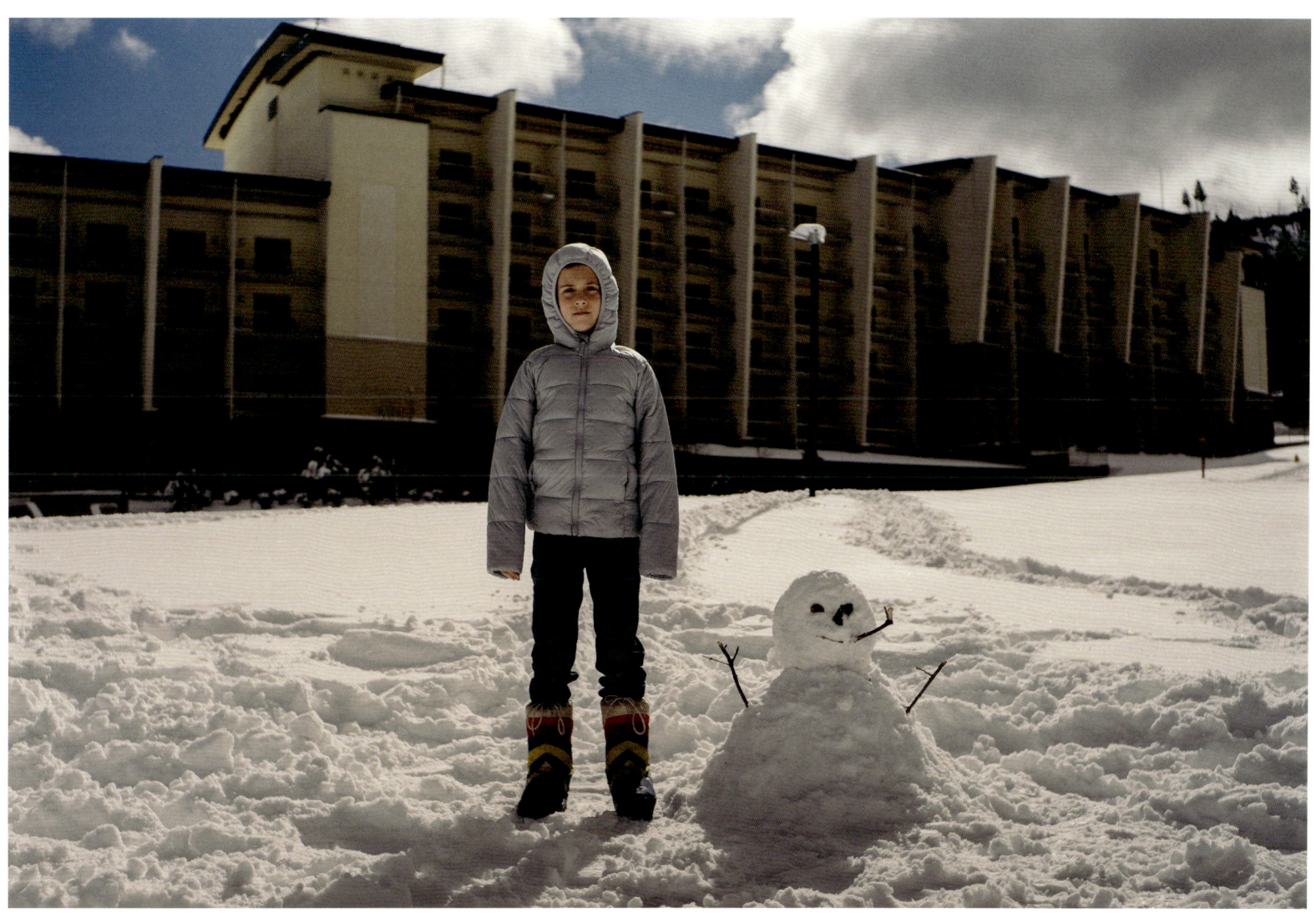

FIVE DAYS AFTER WE MET, MY NEW FAMILY LEFT WITHOUT ME FOR A SKI TRIP IN RED RIVER. I WAITED NINE YEARS FOR THE NEXT GOOD SNOW.

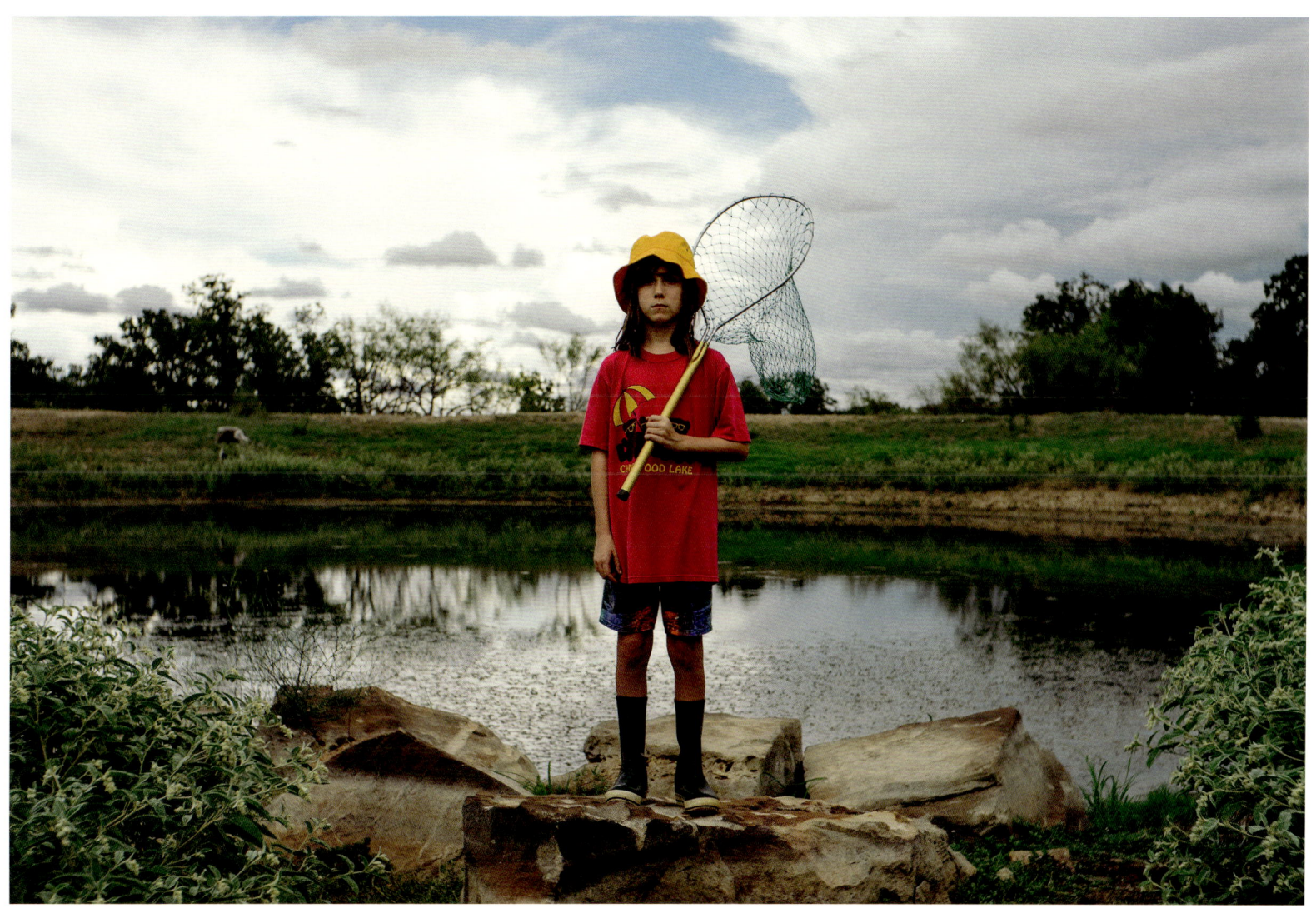

MY GRANDFATHER TAUGHT ME HOW TO FISH WITH A STRING AND A PAPERCLIP.
LIFE WAS GOING TO TEACH ME THAT IT WOULDN'T ALWAYS BE SO SIMPLE.

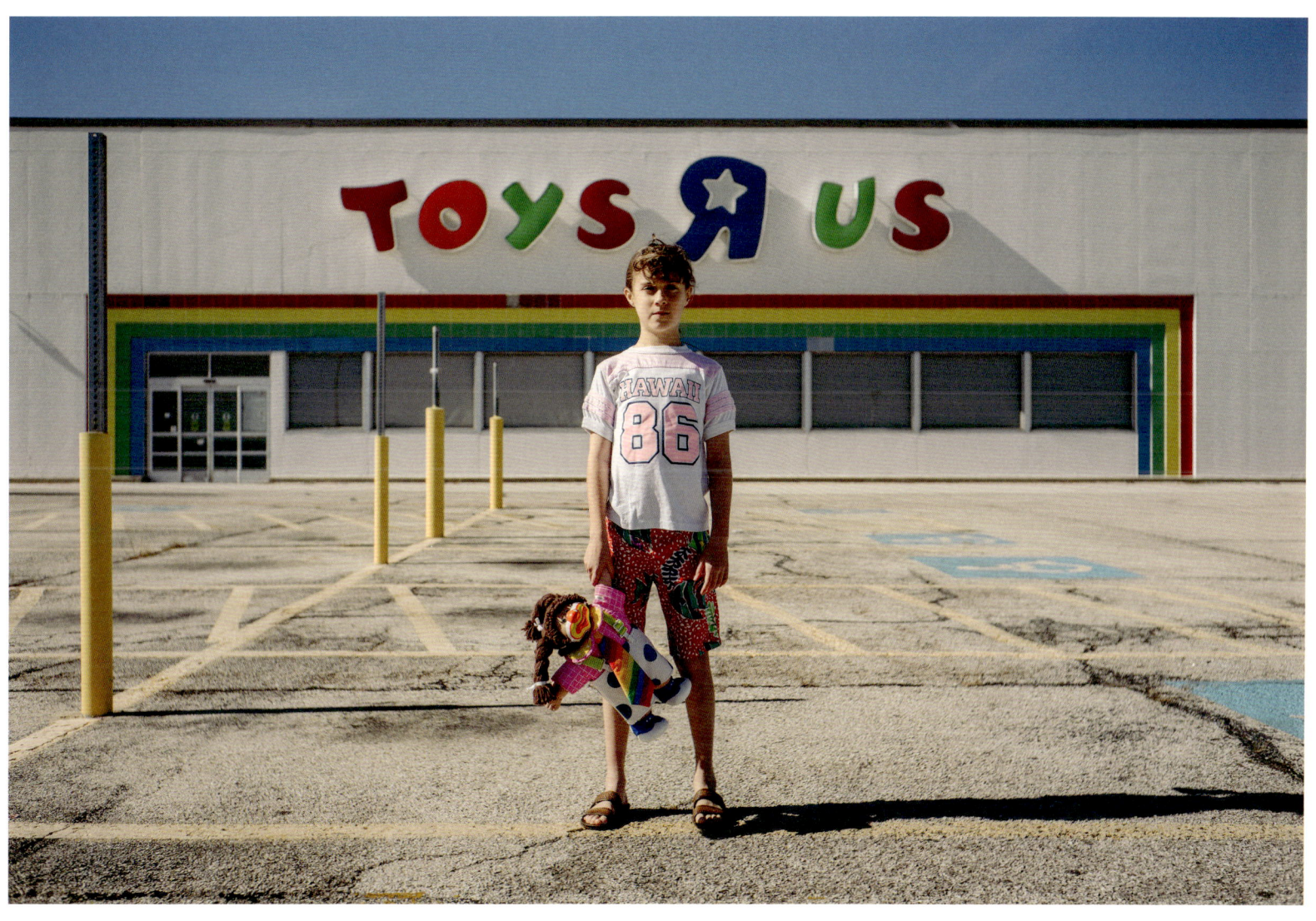

CABBAGE PATCH KIDS WERE OUR COMPROMISE: MY MOM GOT TO BUY ME A DOLL,
AND I GOT TO TALK TO SOMEONE ABOUT HOW IT FELT TO BE ADOPTED.

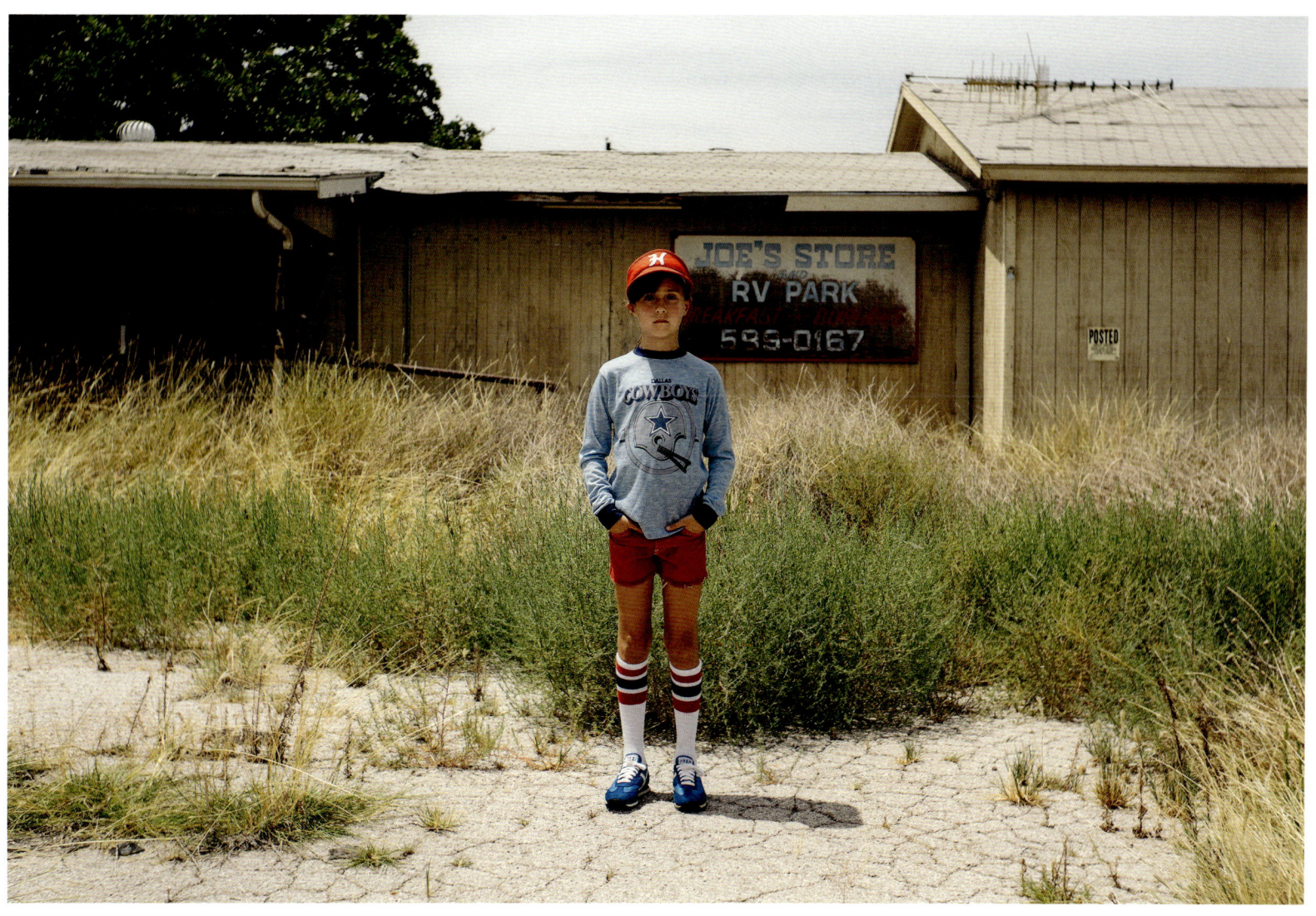

CAN I WEAR MY PAJAMAS TO THE STORE? YES.
CAN I BUY 18 SLO POKES AND EAT THEM FOR DINNER? YES.
WILL YOU ALWAYS LOVE ME, NO MATER WHAT? YES.
BECAUSE GRANDMOTHERS NEVER SAY NO.

WE ALL HAVE OUR CHILDHOOD HEROES, THOUGH PISTOL
PETE MARAVICH DIED OF A SUDDEN HEART ATTACK,
AND ANN RICHARDS WOULD LATER SUCCOMB TO
CANCER.

BUT RAMONA QUIMBY, AGE 8? SHE'LL LIVE FOREVER.

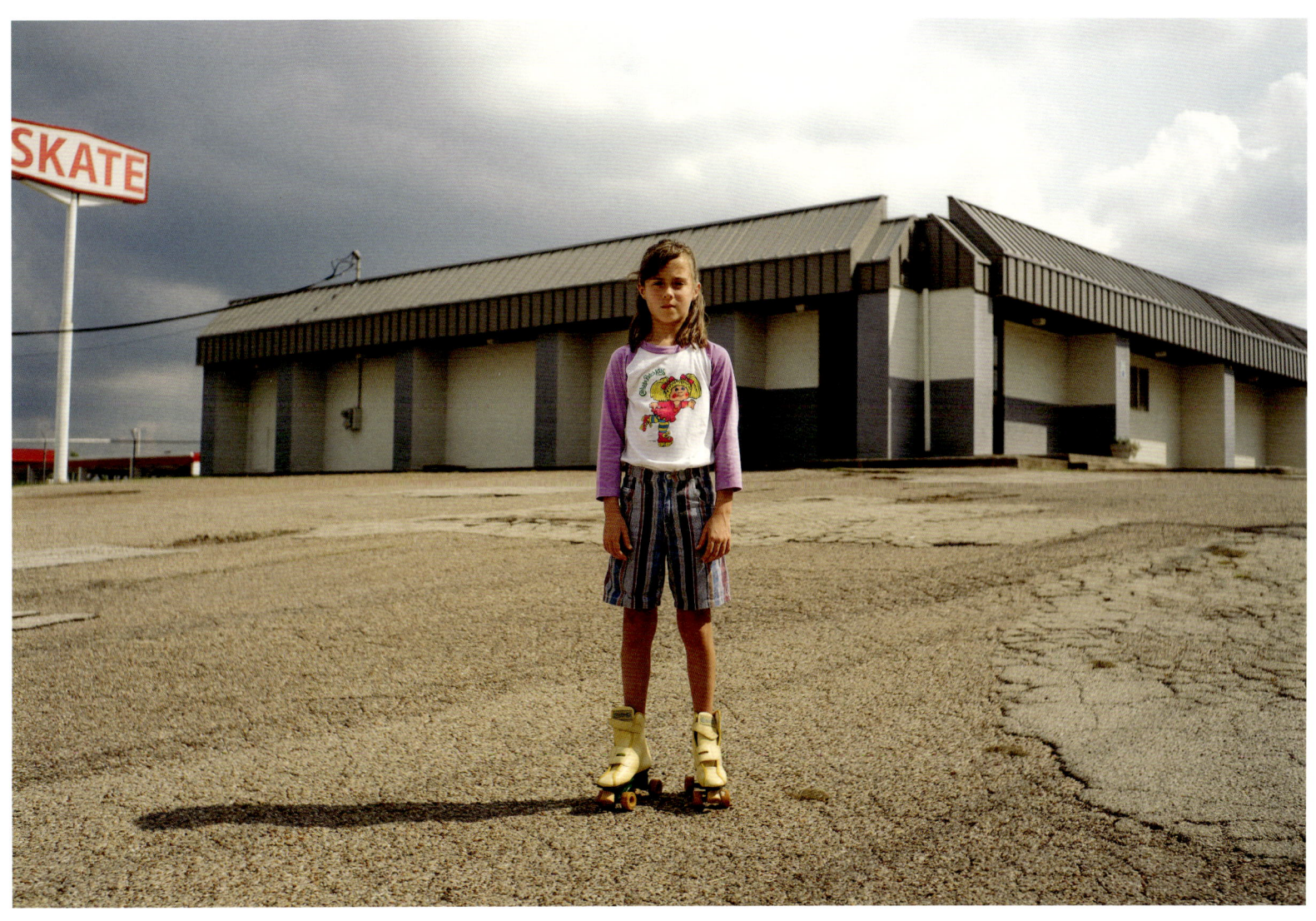

MY BIRTHDAY'S IN DECEMBER, SO I CELEBRATED MY HALF BIRTHDAY IN JUNE,
UNDER THE LIMBO STICK, ALL AROUND THE LIMBO CLOCK.

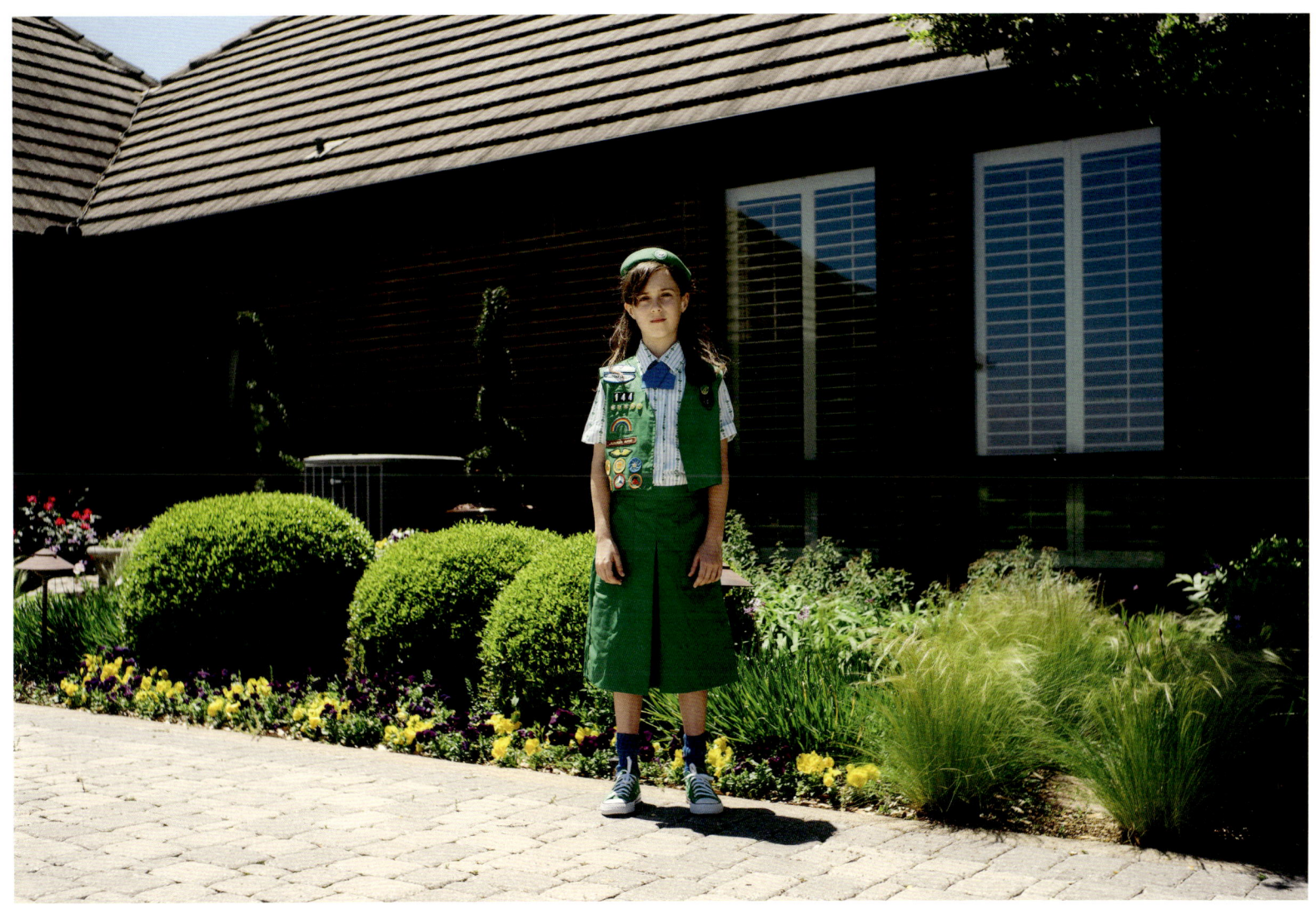

THERE WASN'T A "FUNCTIONING IN A DYSFUNCTIONAL FAMILY" BADGE
OR I WOULD'VE EARNED THAT ONE, TOO.

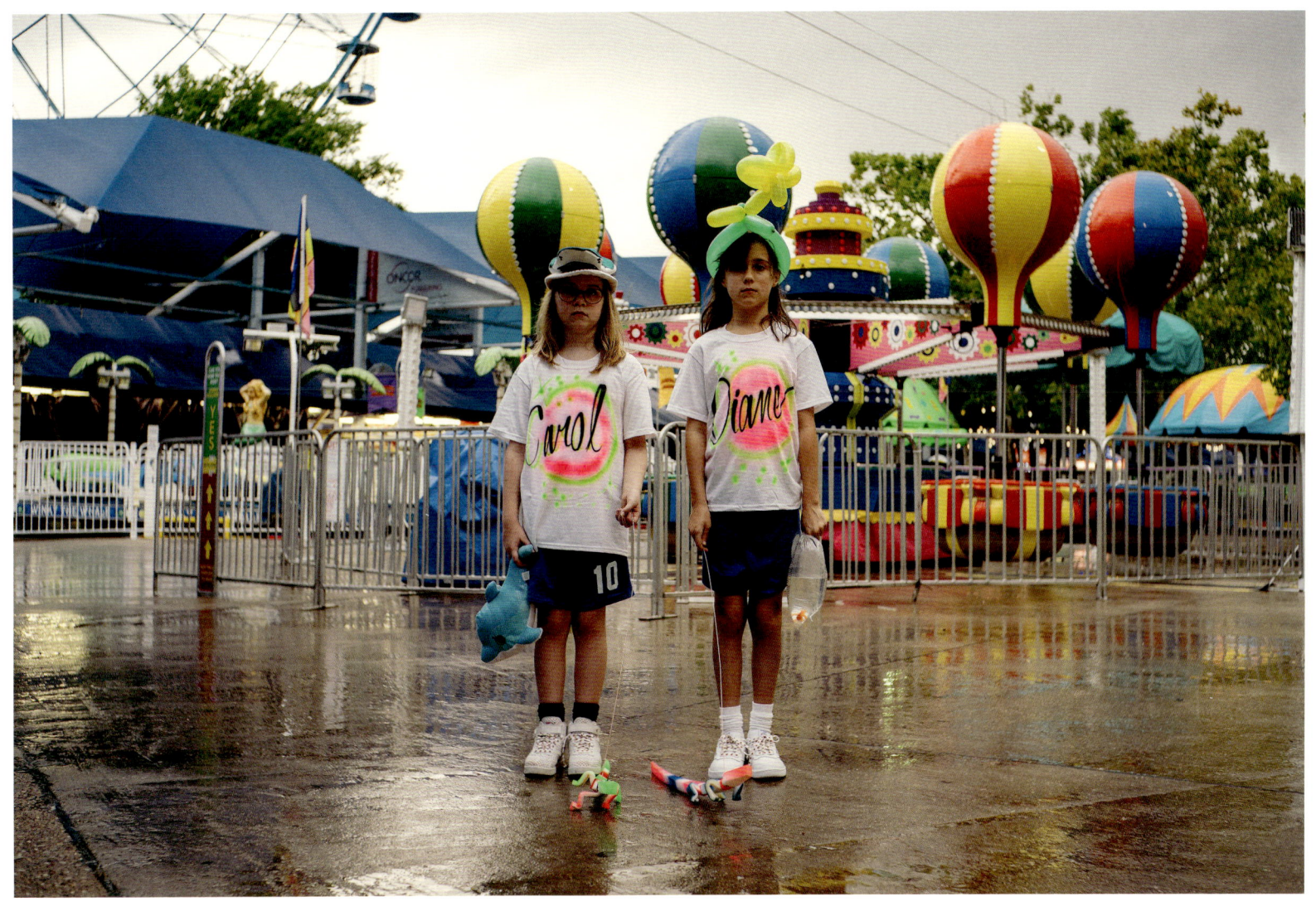

I WON A GOLDFISH EVERY YEAR, AND EVERY YEAR I NAMED HIM ABRAHAM.
I STILL MISS HIM EVERY DAY. ALL EIGHT OF HIM.

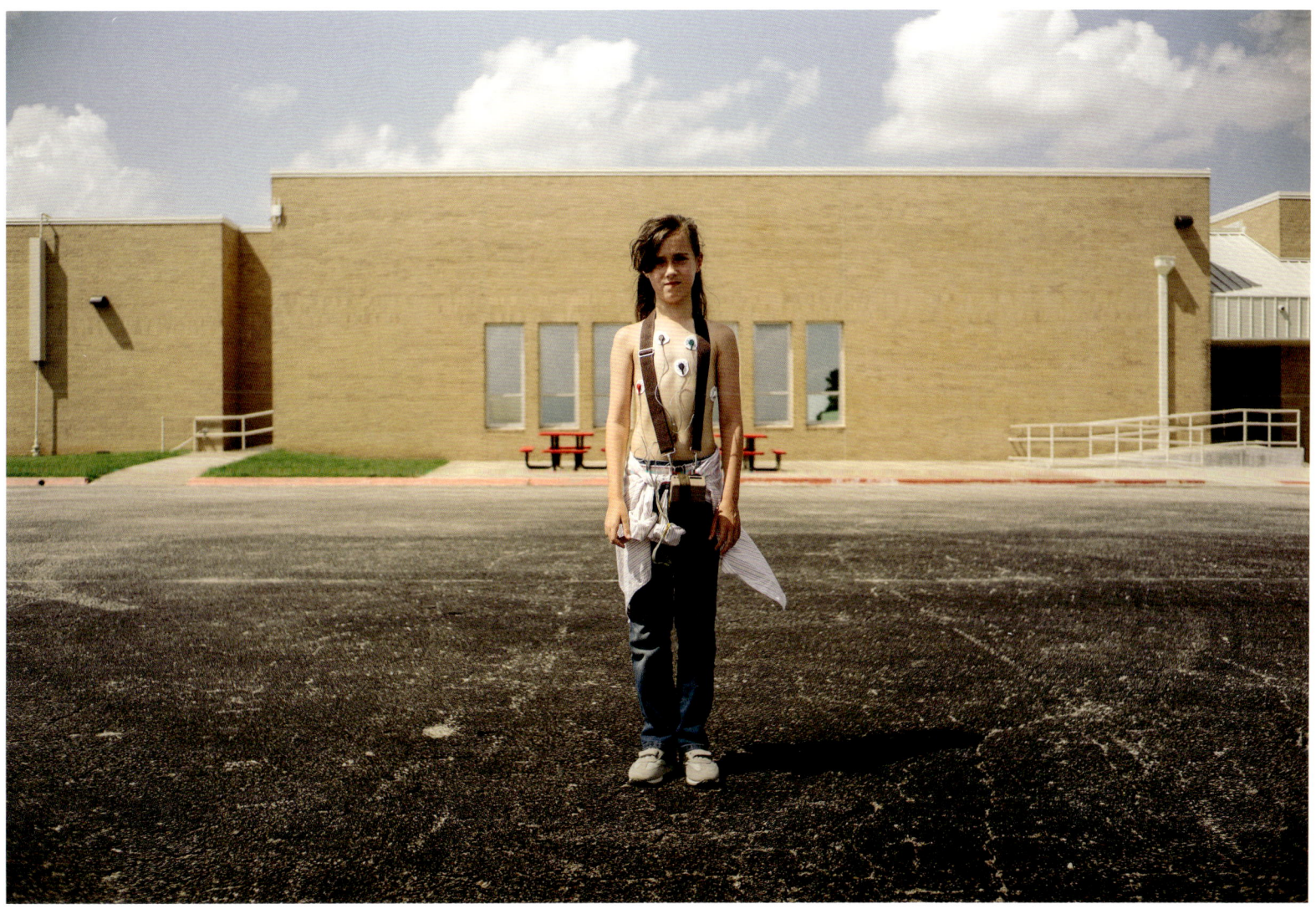

THE DOCTOR SAID NOT TO WORRY ABOUT WHAT OTHER PEOPLE MAY THINK AND TO GO ABOUT MY NORMAL LIFE. BUT I DON'T THINK I'VE FIGURED OUT HOW TO DO THAT EVEN STILL.

I INHERITED MY GREAT-GRANDMOTHER'S TRAIN CASE THAT YEAR, A BEAUTIFUL BLUE LEATHER BOX WITH GOLD LATCHES, AN INLAID SHELF FOR ESSENTIAL COSMETICS, AND A GOODLY SIZED MIRROR. EVERYTHING A TRAVELING WOMAN COULD NEED.

MY ROCK COLLECTION FIT PERFECTLY.

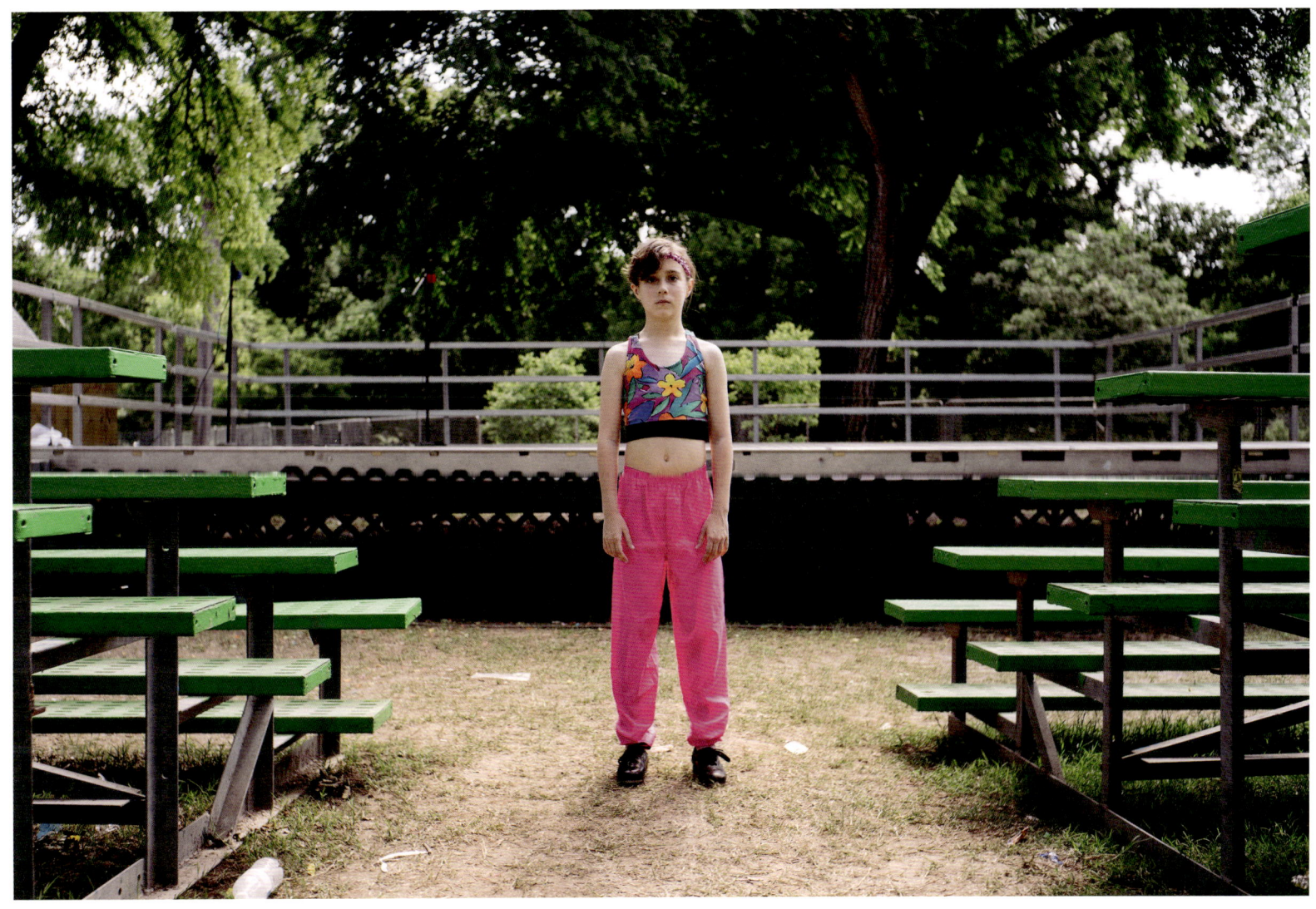

WE DANCED AT MAYFEST DESPITE THE TORNADO WARNING.
WE DANCED AT CHERRY PARK DESPITE THE HEAT ADVISORY.
I WORE MAKEUP AND SMILED LIKE A GOOD LITTLE GIRL DESPITE IT ALL.

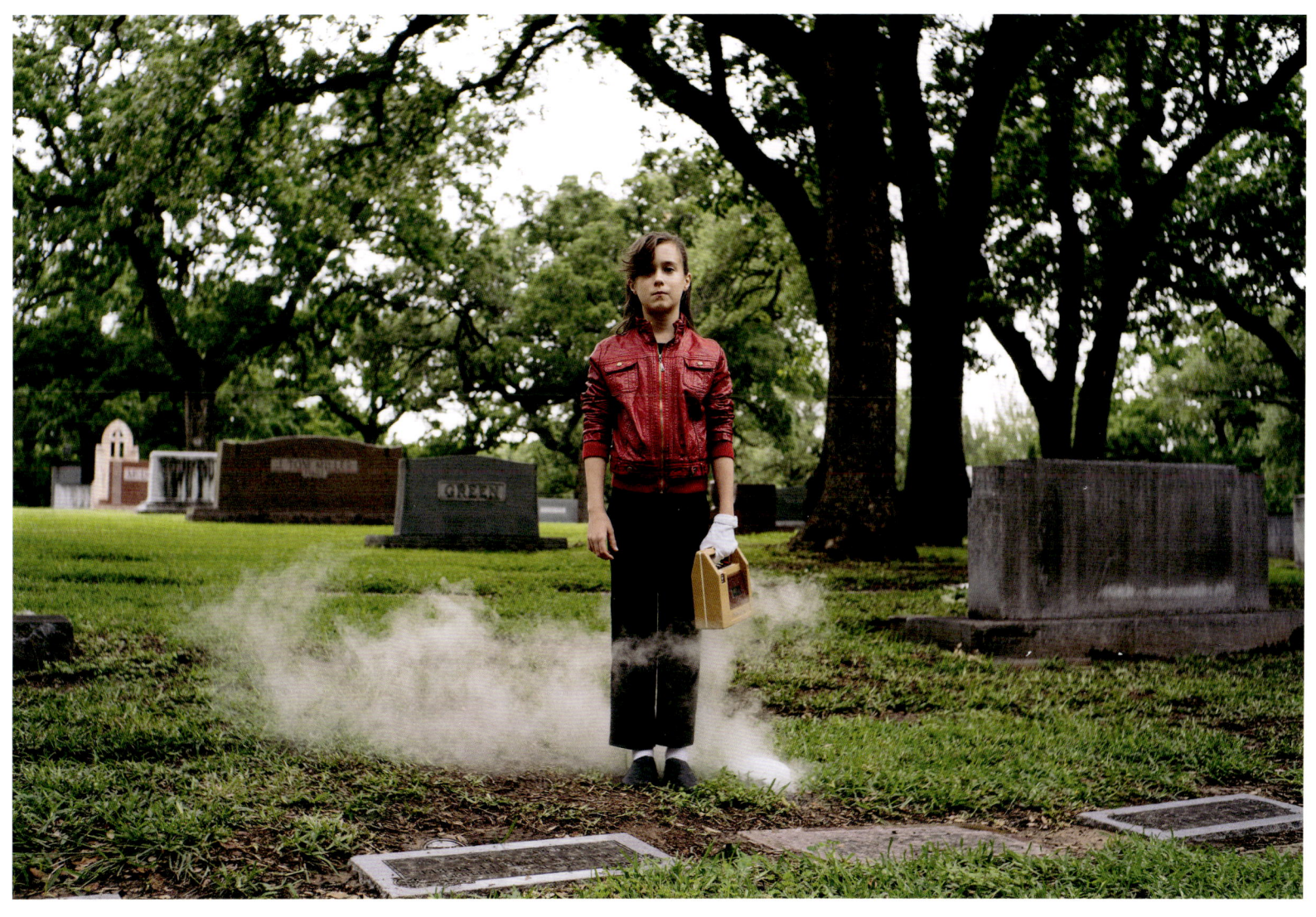

I WASN'T BAD, BUT I WAS NOTORIOUS FOR INTERRUPTING MY PARENTS' DINNER PARTIES WITH A WELL-REHEARSED PERFORMANCE OF MICHAEL JACKSON'S THRILLER, CULMINATING IN A MOON WALK ALONG THEIR FRESHLY PLEDGED COFFEE TABLE. IT WAS A FRESH SHINE, EVERY TIME.

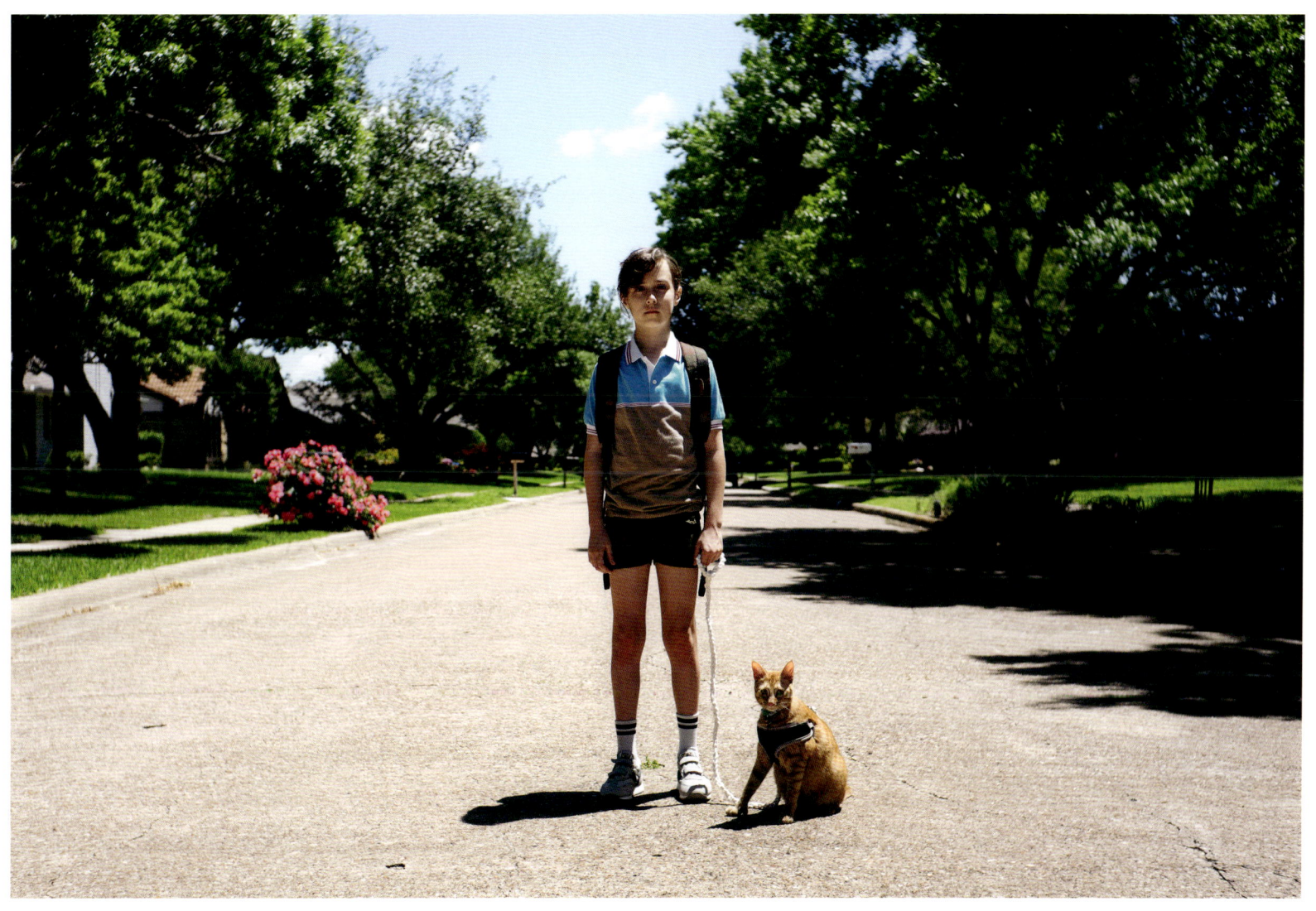

APRICOT ESCAPED WHEN WE MOVED ACROSS TOWN.

I DIDN'T KNOW ENVY UNTIL HE LEFT A SECOND TIME AND NEVER CAME BACK.

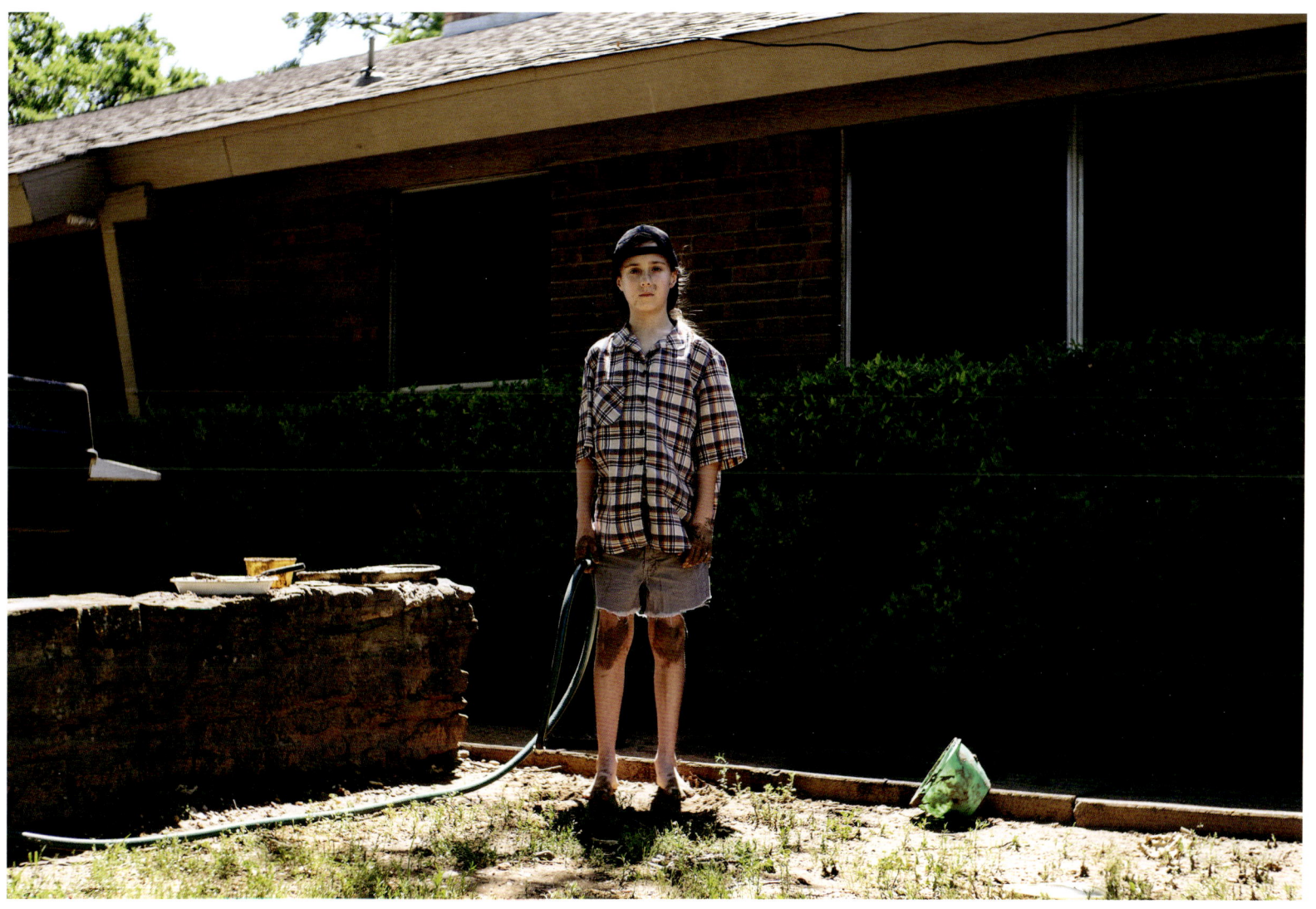

THE KEY TO MUDPIES WAS IN THE MIXTURE, ADDING JUST ENOUGH WATER
TO MAKE THE EARTH PLIABLE (THOUGH NOT NECESSARILY PALATABLE).
THE KEY TO EVERYTHING ELSE? BENDING, BUT NOT BREAKING.

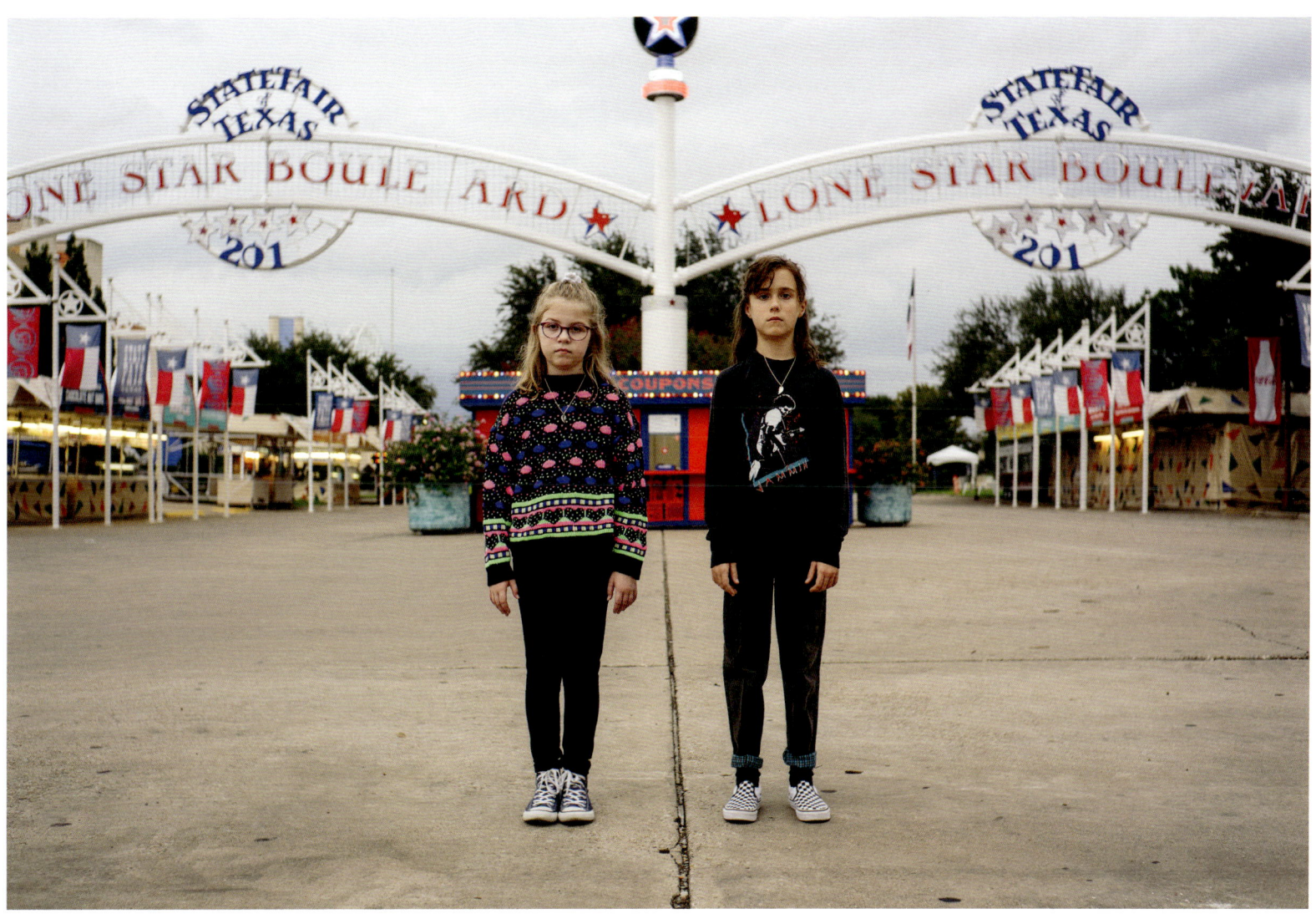

GOING TO THE STATE FAIR EACH YEAR DIDN'T MAKE EVERYTHING BETTER.
HAVING A BEST FRIEND DID.

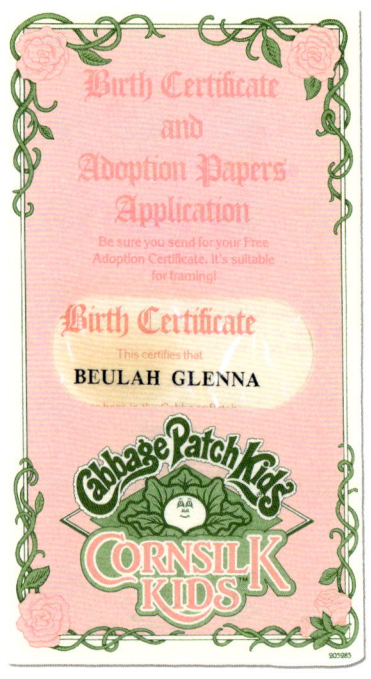

**Birth Certificate**
**and**
**Adoption Papers**
**Application**

Be sure you send for your Free
Adoption Certificate. It's suitable
for framing!

**Birth Certificate**

This certifies that

**BEULAH GLENNA**

*Cabbage Patch Kids*
**CORNSILK KIDS**

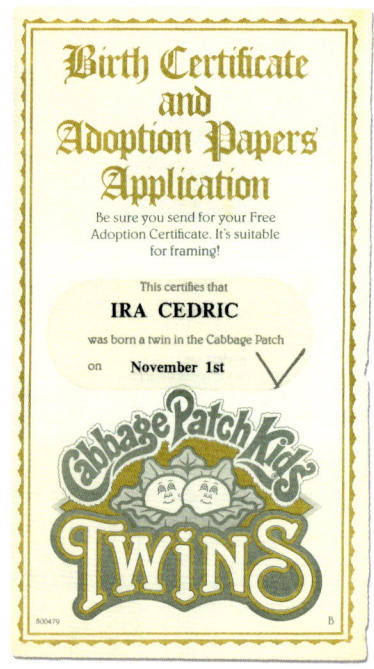

**Birth Certificate**
**and**
**Adoption Papers**
**Application**

Be sure you send for your Free
Adoption Certificate. It's suitable
for framing!

This certifies that

**IRA CEDRIC**

was born a twin in the Cabbage Patch

on      **November 1st**

*Cabbage Patch Kids*
**TWINS**

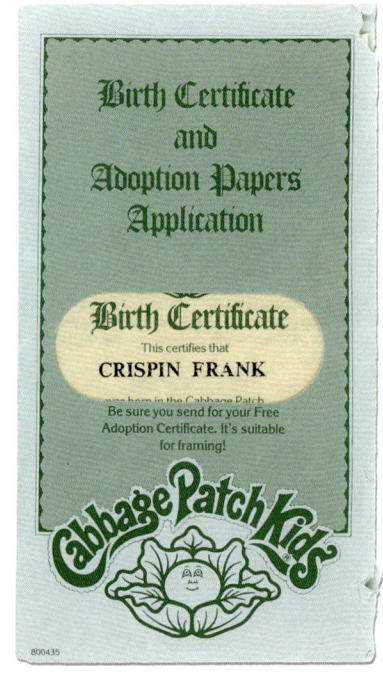

**Birth Certificate**
**and**
**Adoption Papers**
**Application**

**Birth Certificate**

This certifies that

**CRISPIN FRANK**

was born in the Cabbage Patch
Be sure you send for your Free
Adoption Certificate. It's suitable
for framing!

*Cabbage Patch Kids*

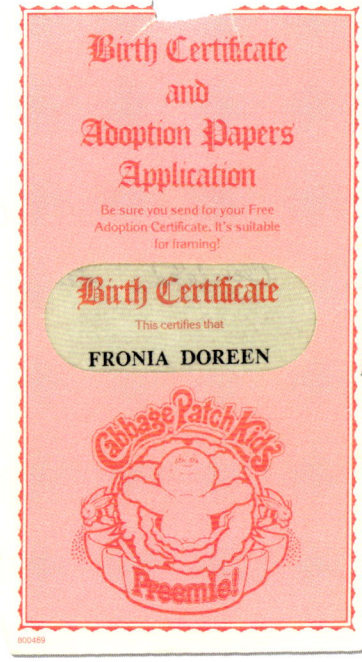

**Birth Certificate**
**and**
**Adoption Papers**
**Application**

Be sure you send for your Free
Adoption Certificate. It's suitable
for framing!

**Birth Certificate**

This certifies that

**FRONIA DOREEN**

*Cabbage Patch Kids*
**Preemie!**

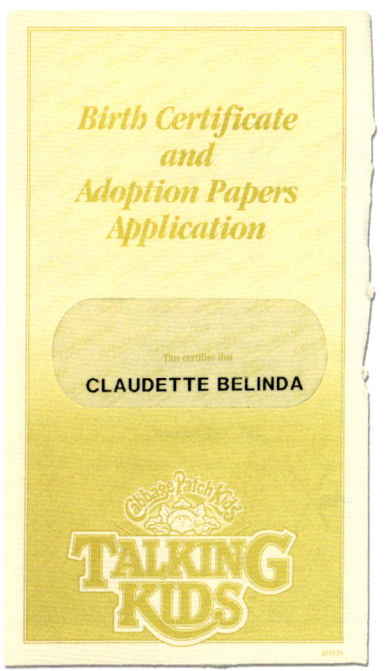

*Birth Certificate
and
Adoption Papers
Application*

This certifies that

**CLAUDETTE BELINDA**

Cabbage Patch Kids
**TALKING KIDS**

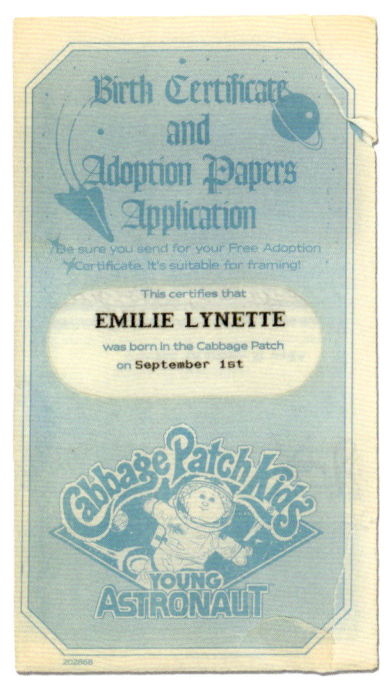

Birth Certificate
and
Adoption Papers
Application

Be sure you send for your Free Adoption
Certificate. It's suitable for framing!

This certifies that

**EMILIE LYNETTE**

was born in the Cabbage Patch

on **September 1st**

Cabbage Patch Kids
**YOUNG ASTRONAUT**

202868

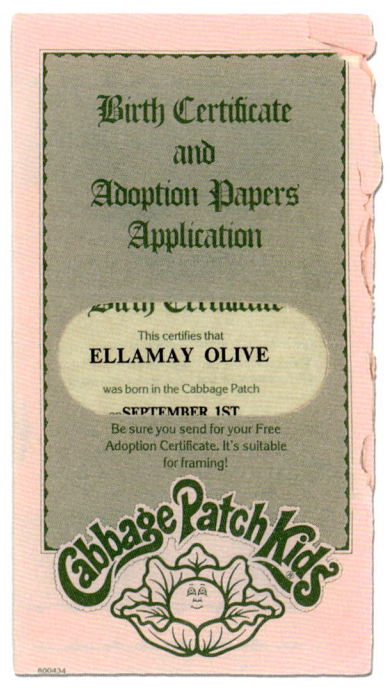

Birth Certificate
and
Adoption Papers
Application

Birth Certificate

This certifies that

**ELLAMAY OLIVE**

was born in the Cabbage Patch

**SEPTEMBER 1ST**

Be sure you send for your Free
Adoption Certificate. It's suitable
for framing!

Cabbage Patch Kids

A00434

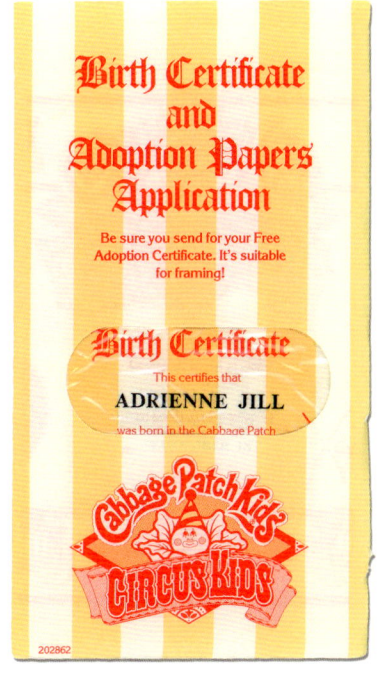

Birth Certificate
and
Adoption Papers
Application

Be sure you send for your Free
Adoption Certificate. It's suitable
for framing!

Birth Certificate

This certifies that

**ADRIENNE JILL**

was born in the Cabbage Patch

Cabbage Patch Kids
**CIRCUS KIDS**

202862

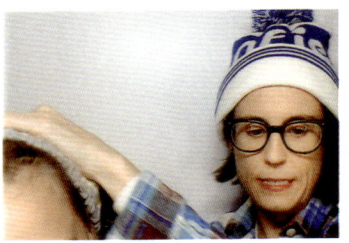
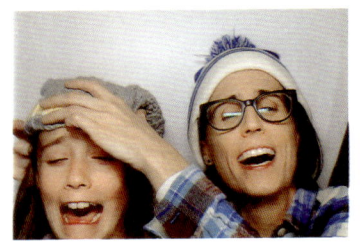
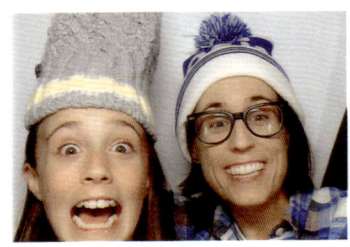
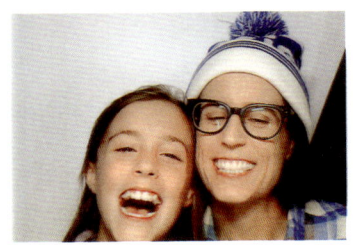
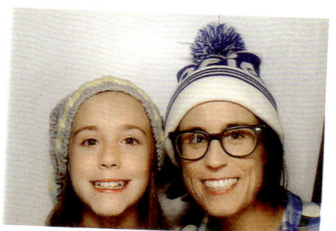
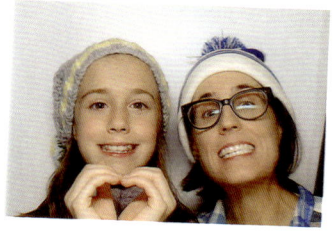
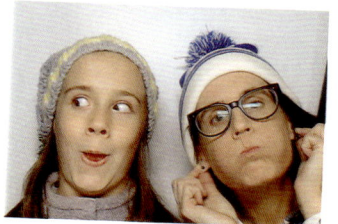
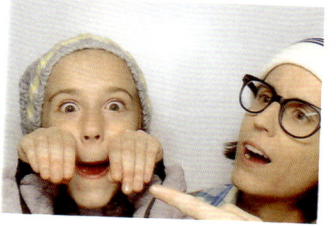

# AFTERWORD

## by Andie McGurren

Coming home from one of the last photo shoots, as I was trying to get comfortable in my outfit, I remember saying to my mom, "These pants are huge. This shirt is too small. Your life was so funny." And it really was.

The funniest shoot was the circus clown one. I had such big feet! How could my mom run away and join the circus in those shoes? I don't want to run away like she wanted to—I want to stay with her and become a magician instead. Or a baker. Or a scientist. Or a professional athlete. Or all of the above.

When I compared a picture of my mom as a kid to one of me dressed up for the photo shoots (I think it was the hobo one), I was surprised by how much we looked alike. Everyone says my mom and I are a lot alike, but her life really was very different from mine. (Her hair was definitely different: she burned my forehead three times trying to curl my bangs!) In the church photo, I feel like the exact opposite of my mom. I'd rather wear a dress than a shirt and pants, but not her. She didn't even want to wear a dress sometimes. But she did want to be a magician, just like me. I thought I knew everything about her already, but as we did these photo shoots, it turns out I didn't. I didn't know that her hair was always crazy. (She didn't really wash it when my grandmother told her to.) Or that her life was sometimes sad, because she didn't talk about that until we started working on the book and I started asking questions. Sometimes I'd ask if we really had to do this, and she'd say, "Yes." What I didn't know was that she didn't always want

to do it either. My mom has been so strong over the years, mentally and physically, and I am so proud of her for making this book. I think working on this with my mom has made my childhood even better. This is way better than just everyday pictures, which is what I would compare the photo shoots to if I had to explain it to someone. Because if it was Halloween, for example, and I was all dressed up and my mom wanted a picture, she would say, "Stand right there . . . scoot a little to your left . . . now come forward." And she'd make sure the sun was in the right place. And that's exactly what she did in the photo shoots, even though the sun was sometimes—it felt like always—in my eyes. "That makes it even more authentic," she would say, and that's what we were going for (she would say).

Overall, it was an interesting experience. My mom's life was very different from mine today, and I'd never thought about that before. I'd never held a gun or worn so much clown makeup (which I really liked, because I really looked like a rodeo clown) or made mudpies or played baseball. But because she did these things, I got to do them, too. It was truly a bonding experience, and though I didn't always want to get up and go shoot, I did it anyway so she could be proud of herself and me, both. I think it will be even more worth it in the end when I have a kid and get to show them this crazy thing I did when I was their age. They probably won't even believe me. They're probably going to ask,"Is that even you?" And I'll say,"Squirrel!" Because I'll probably see a squirrel and not even hear them ask what it was like to be me being my mom.

# ACKNOWLEDGMENTS

A heartfelt thank you to all of my friends, family, colleagues, and students at the University of Texas at Dallas who have loved and encouraged me throughout the course of this project, allowing me to tell my stories, try out a few new jokes, and even borrow their cat. (Great job, Noodle!)

For giving my work space on the walls or championing it through publications and artist lectures, thank you to 500X Gallery; The Amon Carter Museum of American Art; PhotoPlace Gallery and Elizabeth Avedon; Edward Brown and *Fort Worth Weekly*; SPN Gallery and the University of Texas at Dallas; Vignette Women's Art Fair; Fort Worth Community Arts Center; and the Society for Photographic Education. Thank you to Dr. Sheree Gallagher for contributing just the right essay at just the right time.

To the fantastic team at Daylight Books, thank you for this opportunity, for believing in me (and my stories), and for challenging me to push my creative potential further than I could have ever imagined—to Michael Itkoff for seeing the possibility, Ursula Damm for making it a reality, and Barbara Richard for keeping it grammatically correct. This truly would not have happened without your trust, confidence, and creative visions.

A very special thank you to my forever best friend, Carol, and her daughter, who endured the state fair with me for years (and then all over again) and continues to make my childhood memories worth reliving. To the love of my life, Sheryl, without whom little of this would be possible (literally and emotionally), thank you for the laughs, the critiques, the driving all around town to find huaraches, and the fish-sitting. Especially the fish-sitting.

And lastly, a never-ending thank you to my budding thespian of a daughter, Andie. Words cannot express how much I love you, how proud I am of the person you're becoming, and the overwhelming joy I've experienced while working on this project with you, even when we were trespassing and you couldn't run any faster. Save this book. You'll laugh heartily at it in thirty years. Trust me.

*It takes courage to grow up*
*and become who you really are.*

— E. E. Cummings —

32.3078° N, 64.7505° W

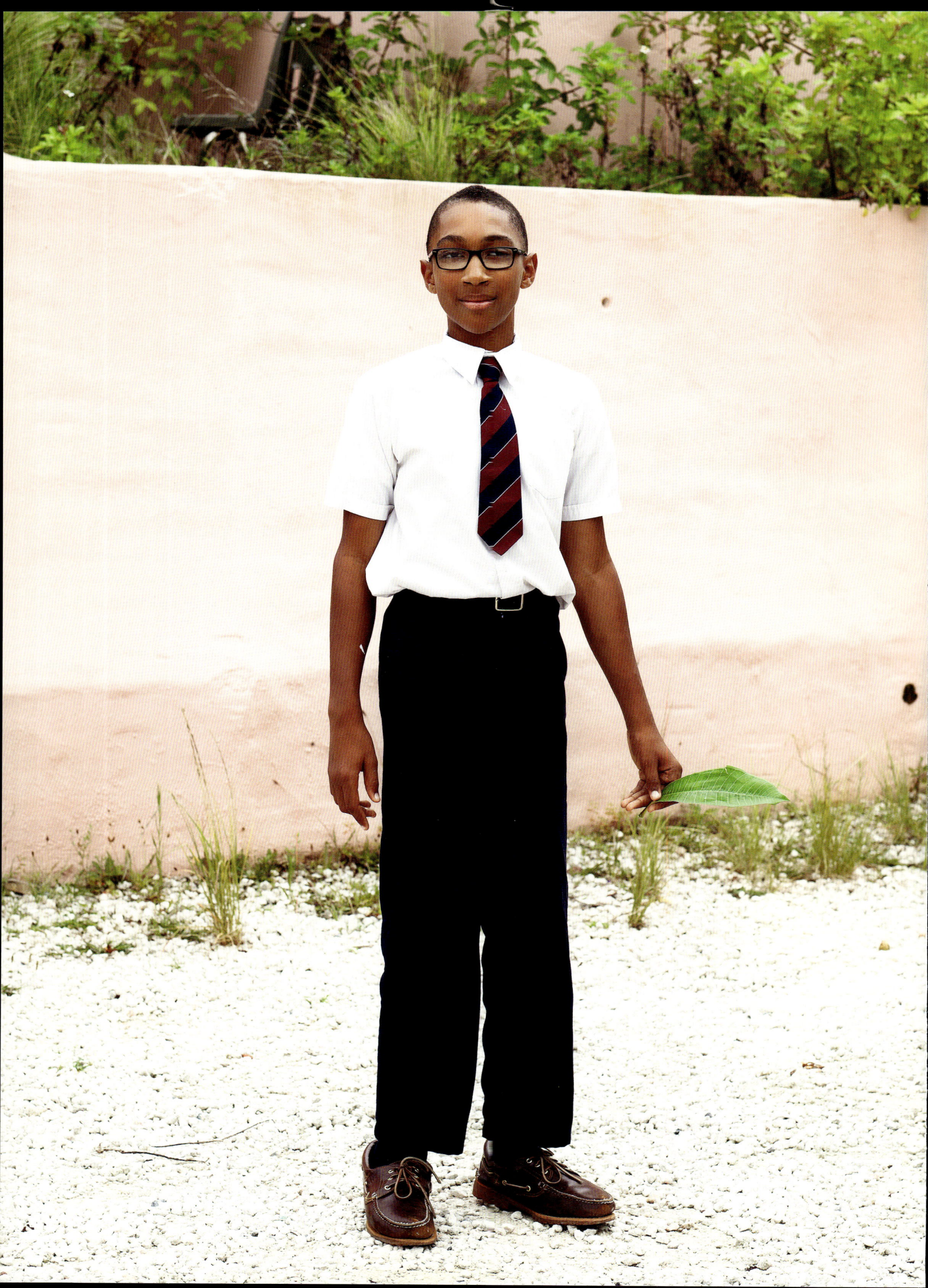

# COMING OF AGE IN WONDERLAND

PHOTOGRAPHS BY DEBRA FRIEDMAN

## PORTRAITS OF TEENAGE BERMUDA

Daylight

Published by Daylight Books
Address: Hillsborough, North Carolina
Cofounders: Taj Forer and Michael Itkoff
Creative director, Daylight Books: Ursula Damm
Designer "Wonderland": Kelsey Blackwell, Studio Blackwell
Copy editor: Elissa Rabellino
Editor: Jay Teitel

Photographs and essay © Debra Friedman 2017 www.debrafriedman.com
Email: radiantphotog@gmail.com
Additional essays by Paul Roth, Tom Butterfield, Dame Pamela Gordon Banks
Poem by Yesha Townsend

Coming of Age in Wonderland, Portraits of Teenage Bermuda, © 2017

ISBN 978-1-942084-42-6

Printed by Artron, China

DAYLIGHT BOOKS
Email: info@daylightbooks.org
Web: www.daylightbooks.org

—

COVER IMAGE
*Friends, Dellwood Middle School, Pembroke Parish*

TITLE PAGE IMAGE
*Boy with Leaf, Dellwood Middle School, hamilton, Pembroke Parish*

*For Bob, who keeps me grounded, and for*
*Nathan, Joseph, and Eli, who keep me aloft.*

—Debra Friedman

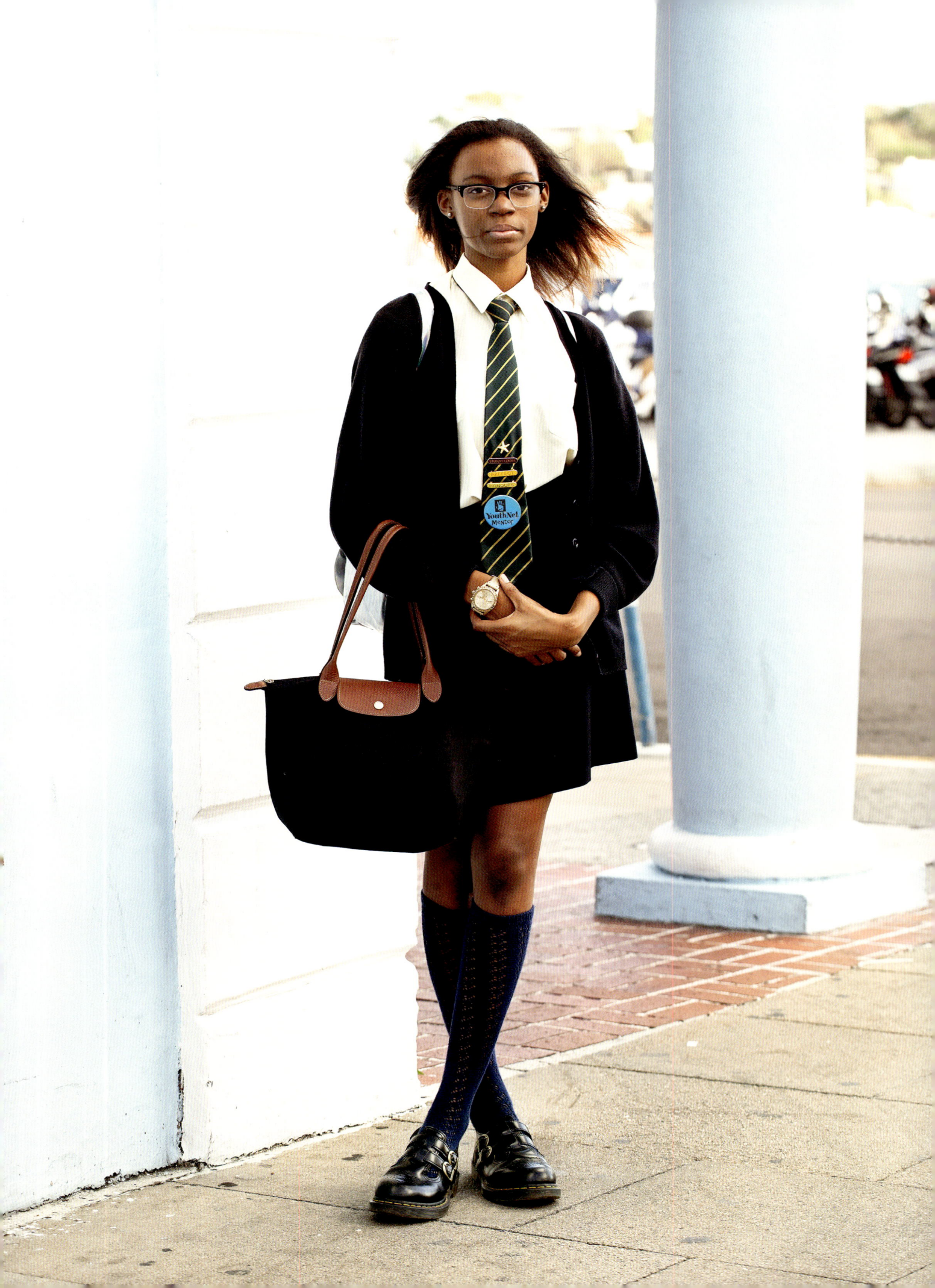

Therefore, we understand Friedman's project best when we see her subjects as representing two realities, theirs and ours. For the children, we imagine, this act of representation is a passing moment, the record of a single instant, seized from the flow of their lives. For the viewer, however, at least for this viewer, our impression is the more resonant and consequential. For us, these portraits represent a longing, a dream of youthful innocence from the nostalgic vantage of adulthood; and a lamentation for the loss that attends our hazy memories of our own passage through childhood.

Caught in the strange space of passing time, their forward motion briefly suspended, Friedman's young Bermudians are figures in photographic amber. The portraitist has beautifully captured their passage through the hopeful traverse of maturation, toward separation from the nest and a future of perfect possibility. With the sadness of impermanence, with the firm knowledge that there's no going back, we watch them make their way, these adolescents in paradise, negotiating the liminal space separating emergence and arrival, becoming and being—following their journey as they finally arrive at whatever comes next.

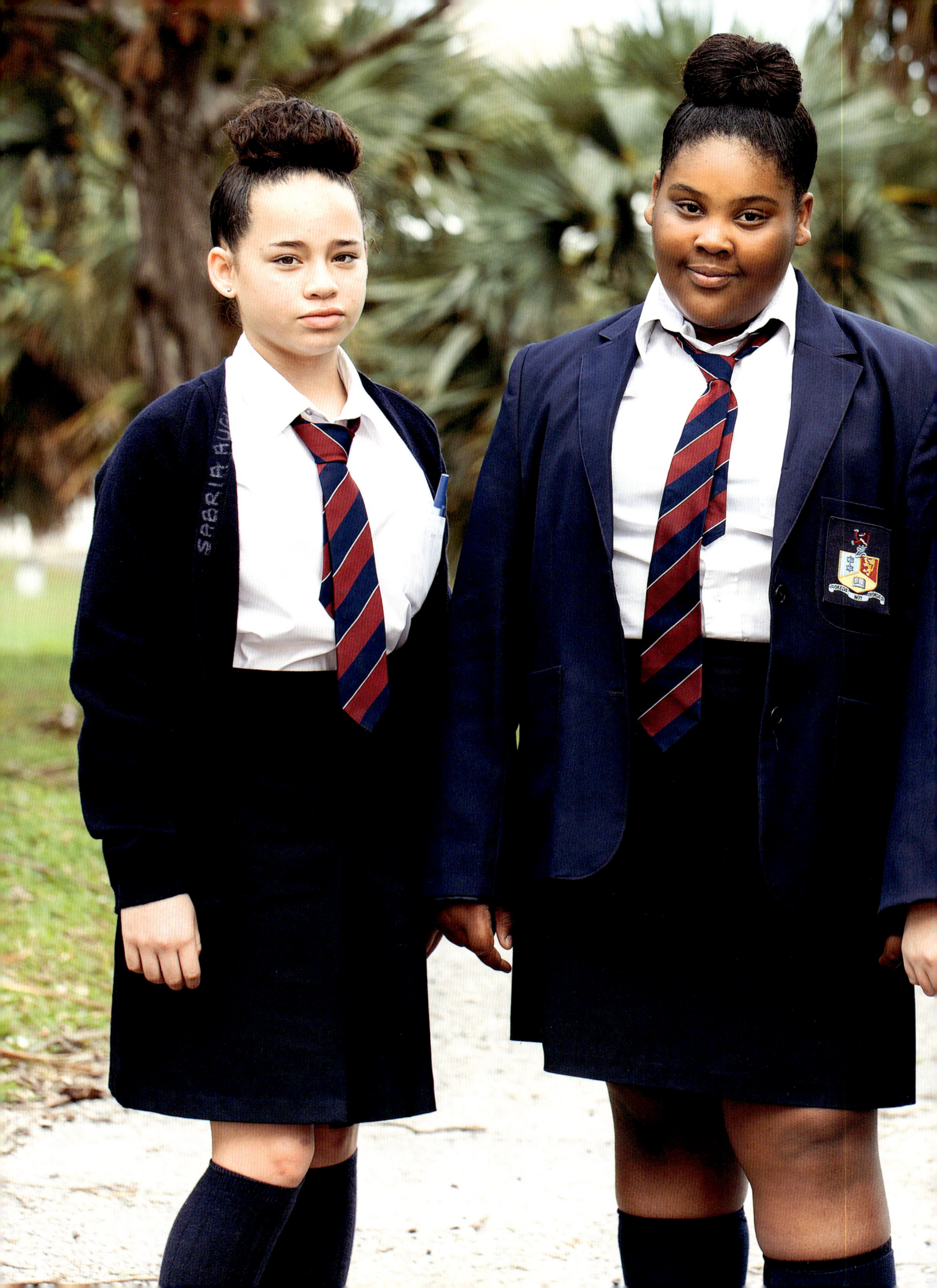

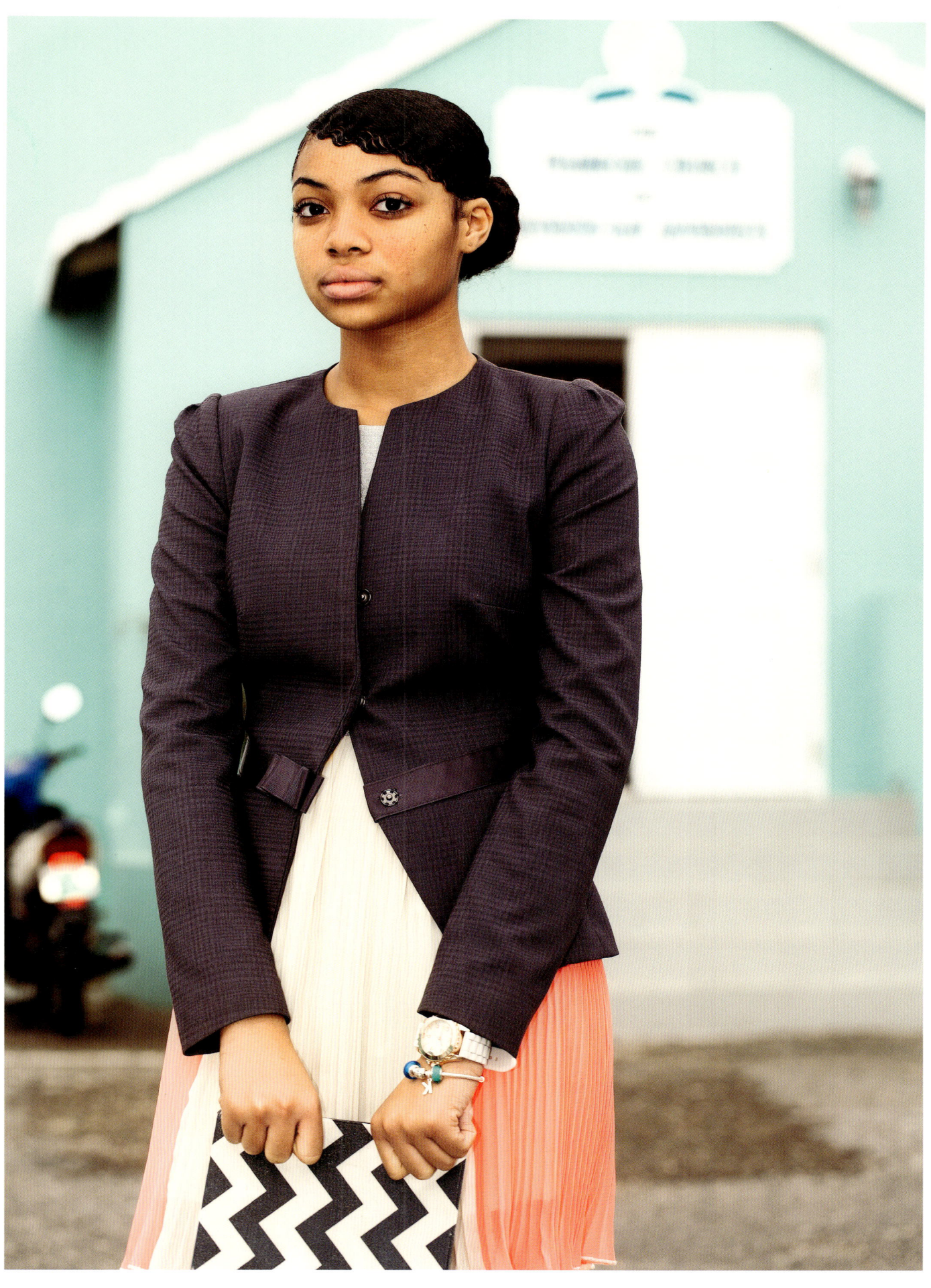

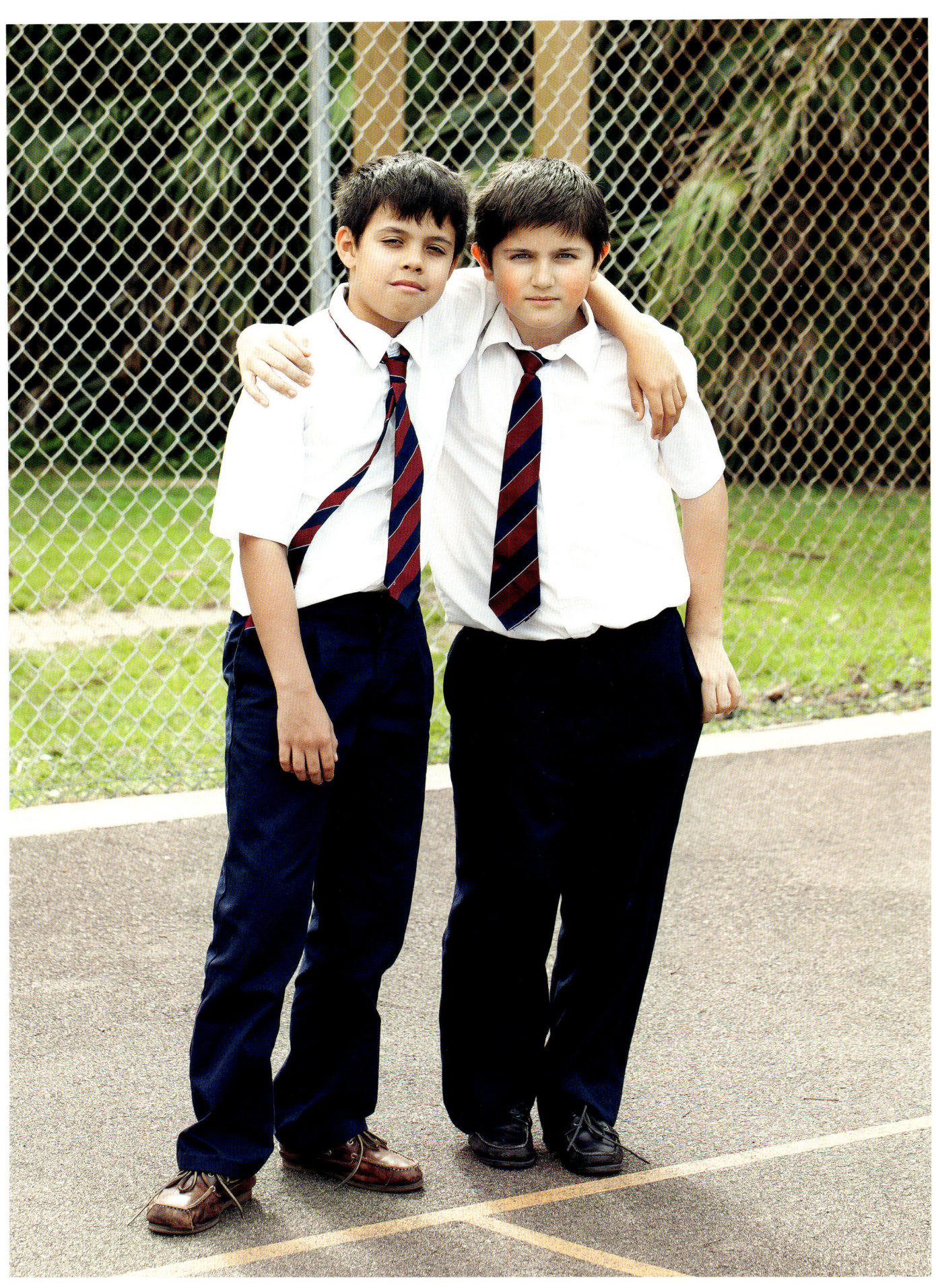

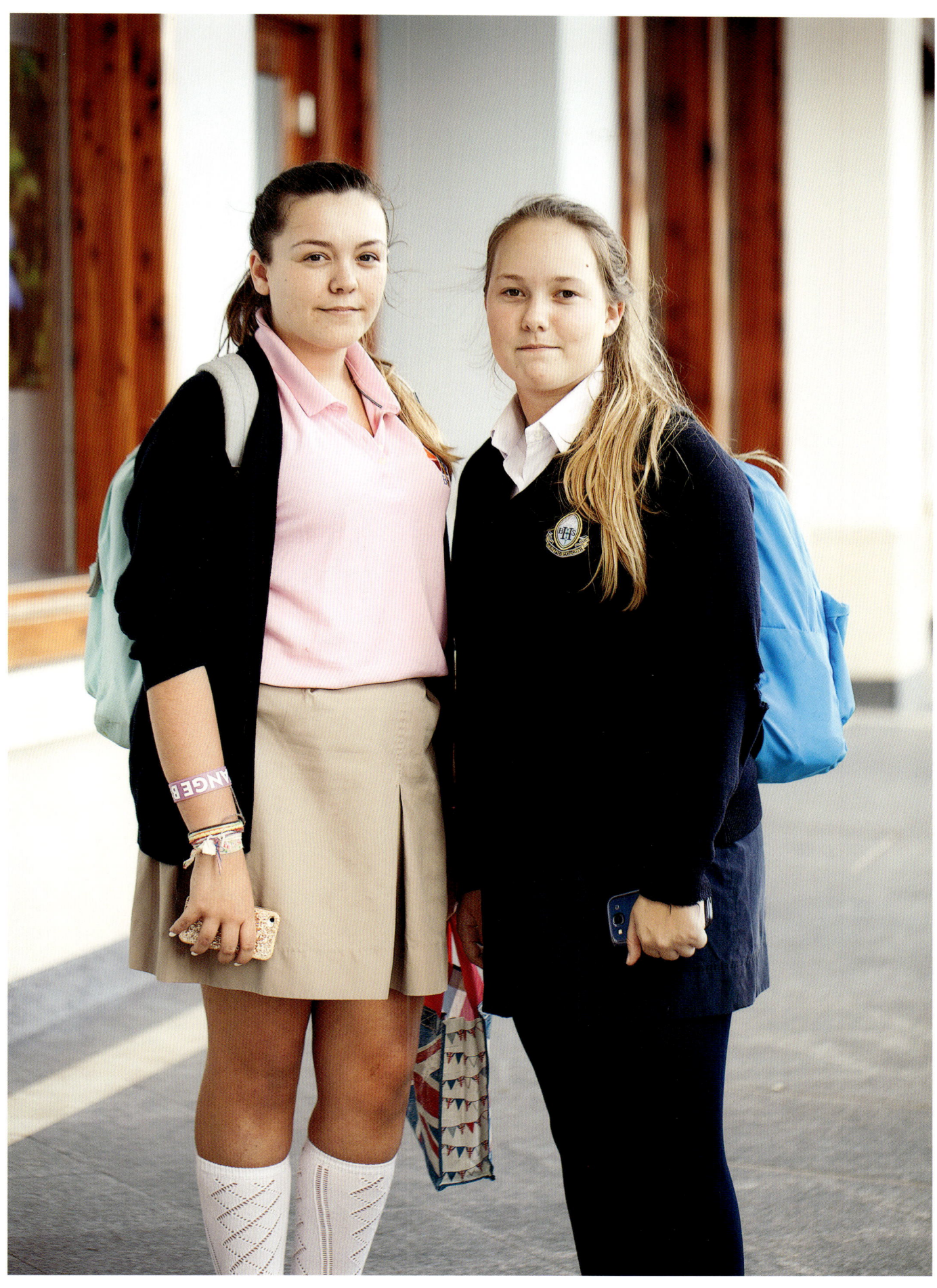

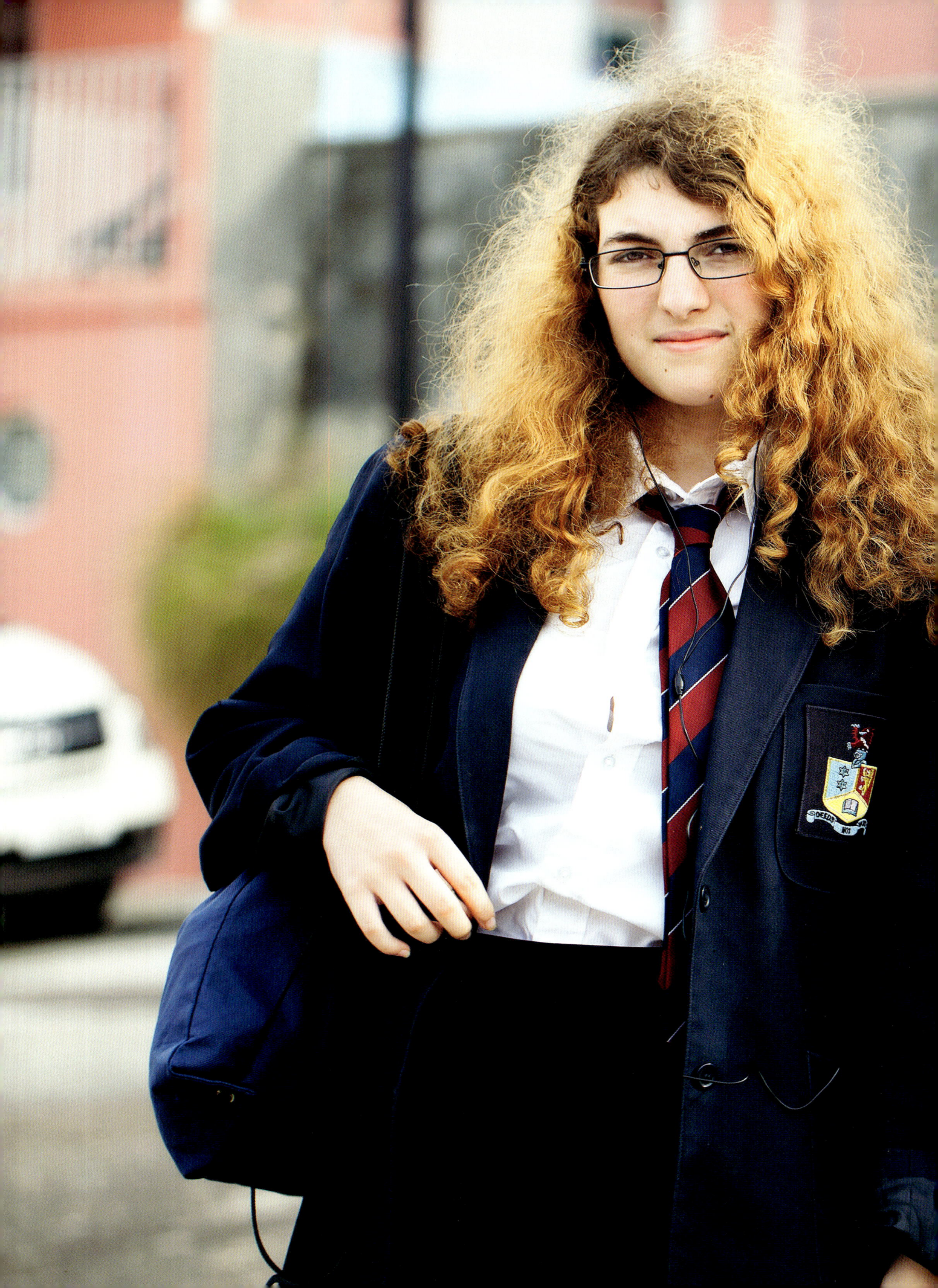

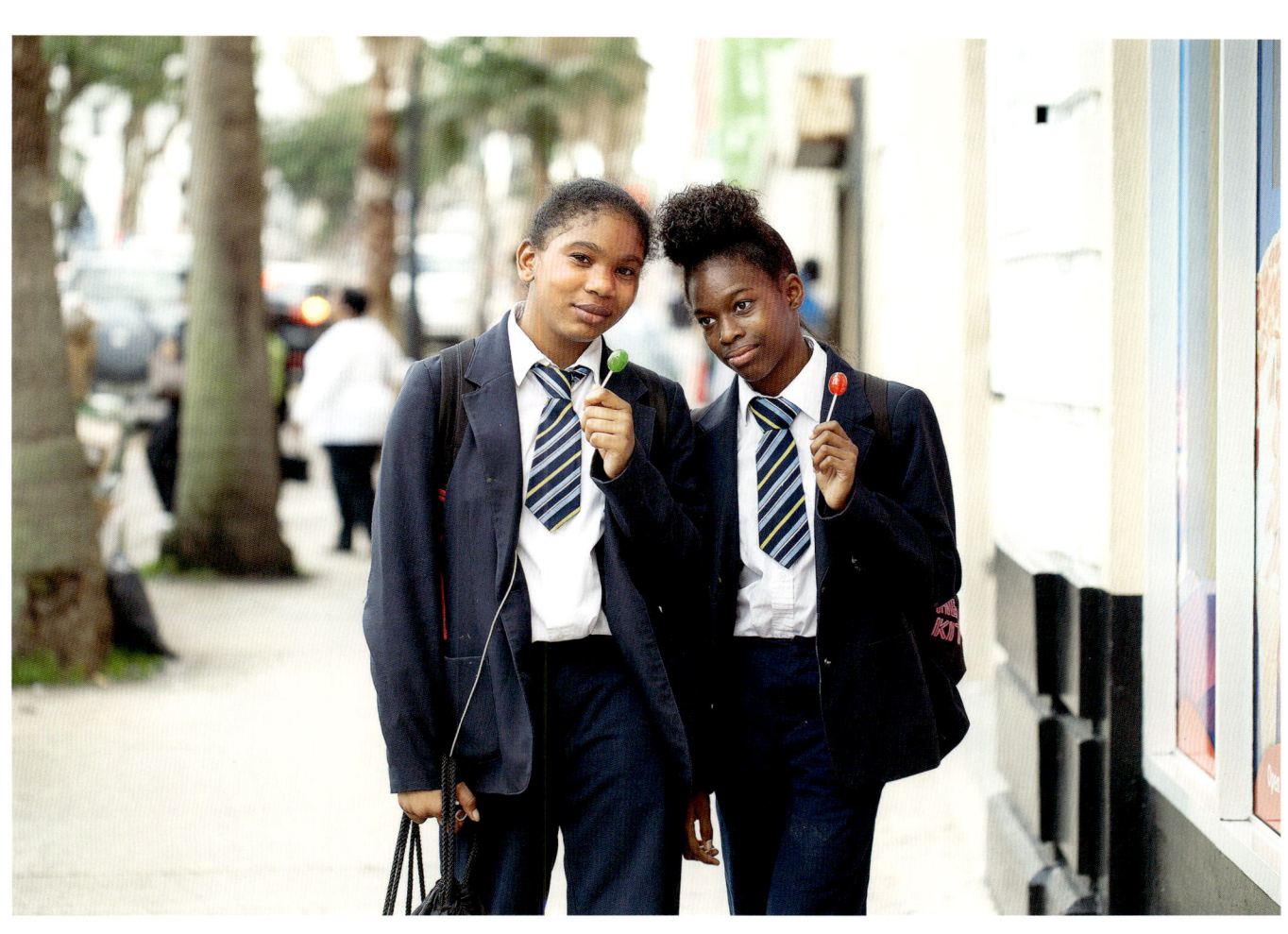

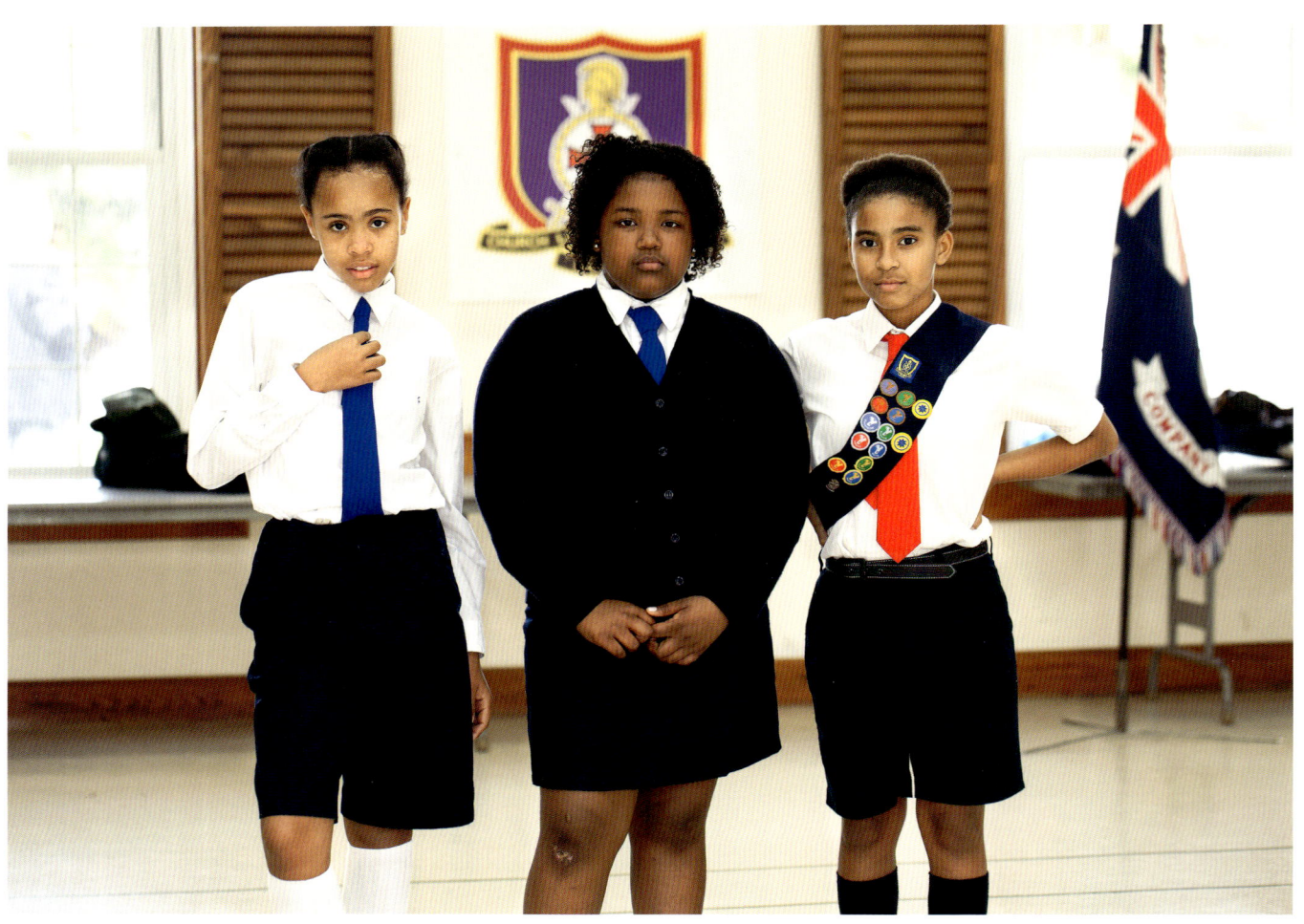

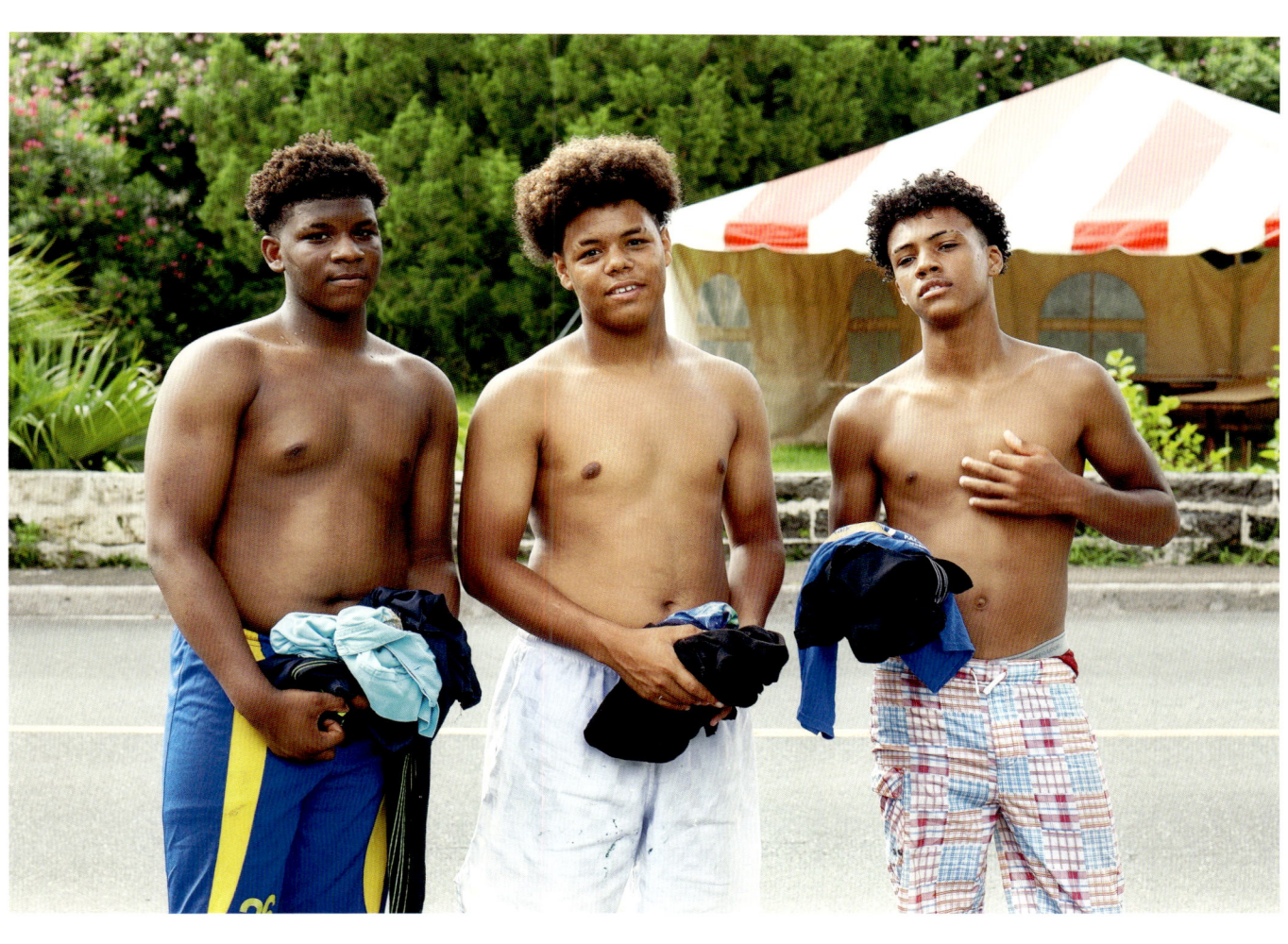

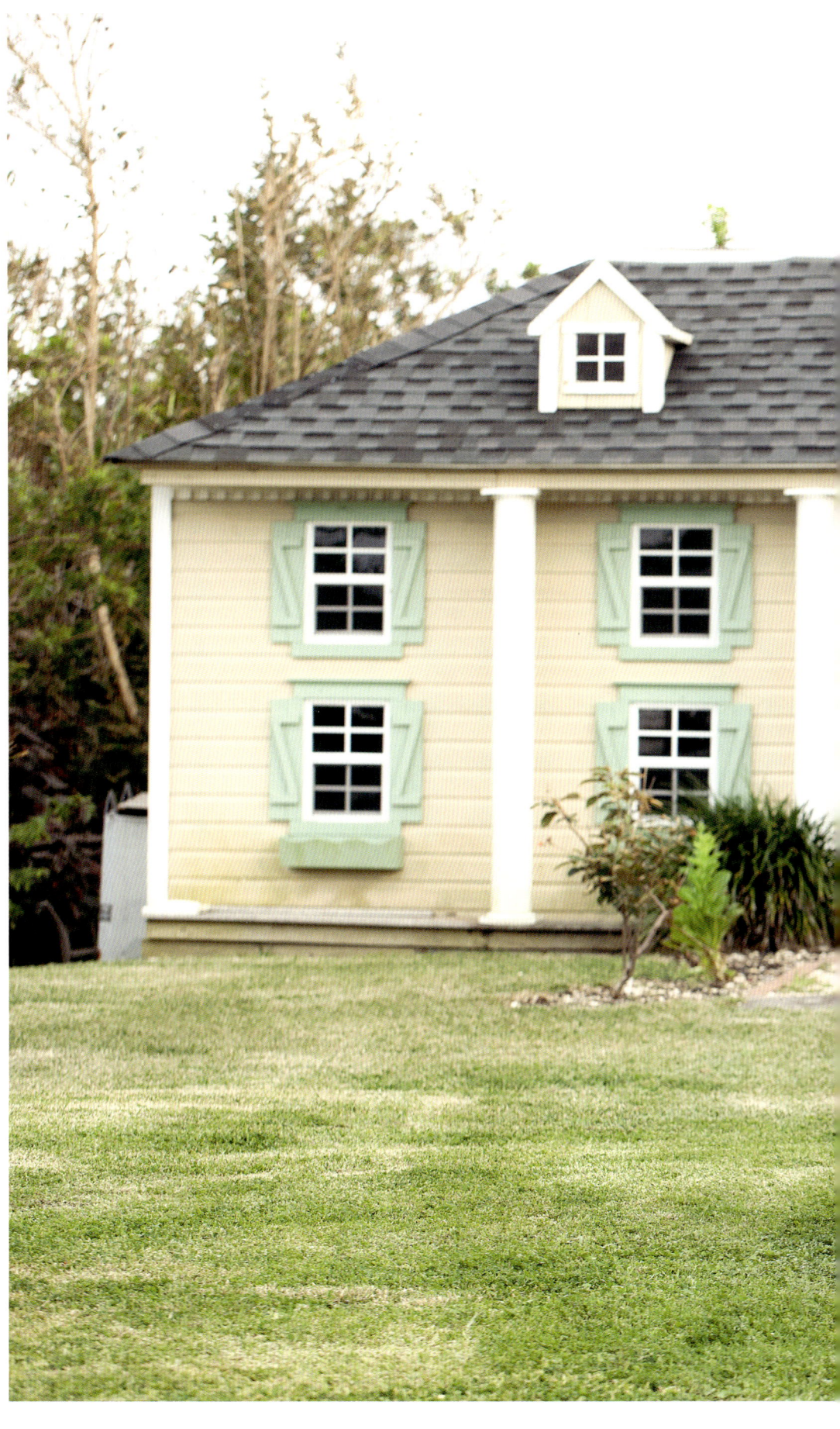

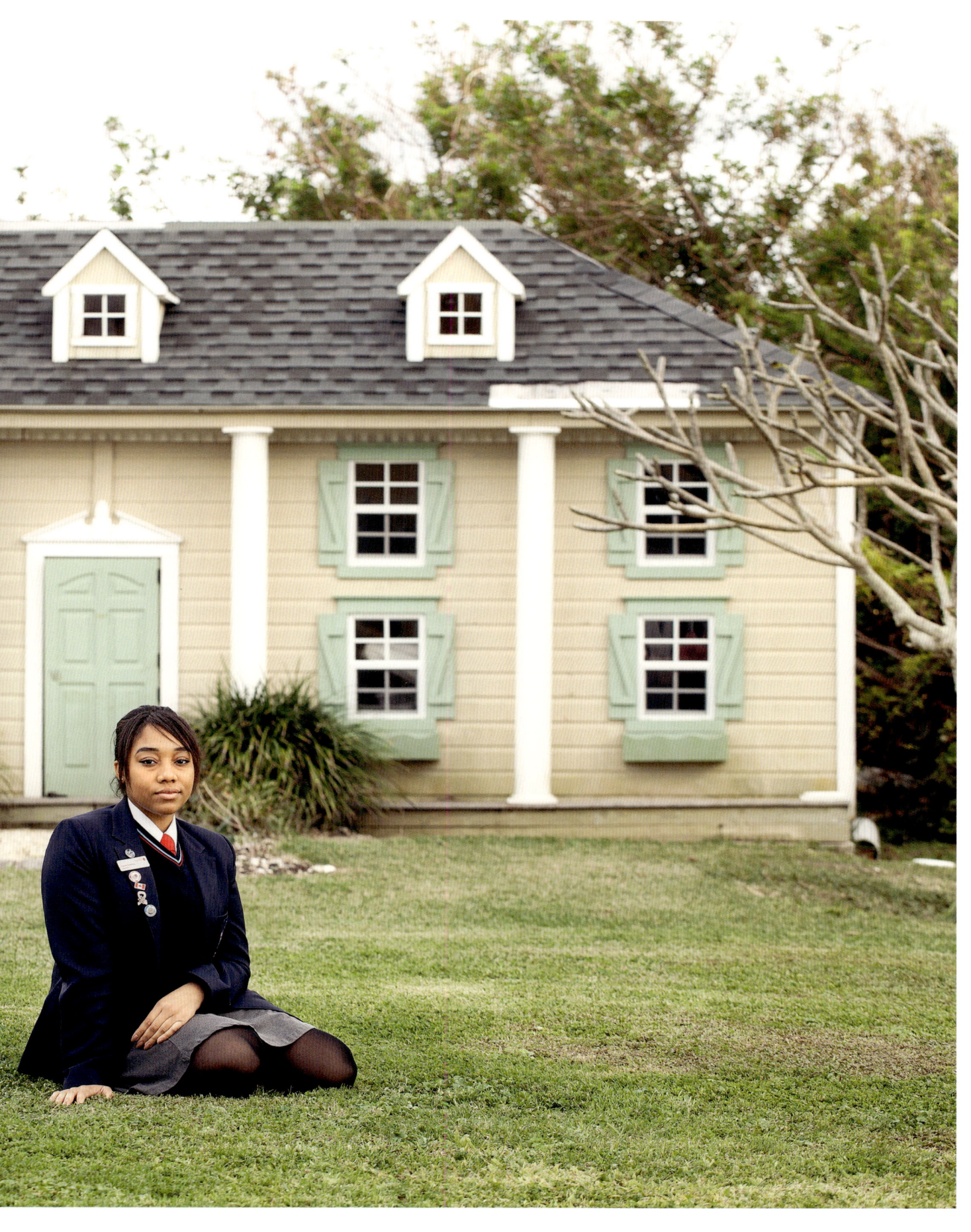

# TAO OF THE BERMUDIAN TEENAGER

YESHA TOWNSEND

I.

make sure your school shirt is ironed and your crash helmet isn't buried under the bed, or a pile of clothes, or resting outside on the side mirror of your bike. ensure you have enough pocket change for gas. buy a bottle of ginger beer on your way to school. check for wayward pencils. be unaware of the arm's-length ocean on your ride. let the sun, guard the top button on your collar. play to the peripherals of the match-me-can leaf. completely disregard your stead in paradise.

II.

sometimes i don't remember being a teenager in Bermuda. my experience in the teens only comes back in flashes of totems, items, and icons that were reappearing fixtures stretching from 11 to 19. ketchup chips and Red Devil soda was my teenage. chicken and beef pies from the Pie Shoppe or Crow Lane Bakery were my teenage. malasadas in the morning before the bus was my teenage. the last few bars of "Ether" when Nas (pun intended) ethered Jay-Z was my teenage. the debate of "which was better?" the champagne, black, or silver Scoopy, was my teenage. things on the precipice of memory; all opposition and balance. equal parts self assurance and smug unawareness. broken between discovery and "things already mastered." i knew everything and nothing, all at once.

III.

there is nothing more magic than jumping from the rocks of Admiralty House, in the spit of summer, when the air is a sustained wet and the sky is eternal. in those moments, do you fly.

IV.

a teenager enters the candy shop at 4:15 pm on a Wednesday. buys sour mats and pixie straws.

a teenager stands at the bus terminal on a Friday morning. she nods her head in succession, her headphones hang like a necklace.

a teenager holds a cahow egg in his palm, there is no-other-such place of this happenstance, he cradles all that is ours.

a teenager stocks shelves at the grocery store, is two years removed from packing groceries, knows to spot the endemic onions.

a teenager races his friend down the street, up the hill, round the bend on two wheels, not even broken on the road yet, speed only being a trace of memory.

a teenager sifts her feet into blush pink sand on the beach, motions to her friends and wades into South shore's waves.

a teenager stands on the summit of Scenic Heights, contemplates the ends of his island home, realizes its small, his small in the belly of the universe.


V.


it's football practice and gombey skanks; fresh sneakers, fresh shirt, fresh press for Cupmatch, Bermuda Day, and Heroes Weekend; it's your first speeding ticket, and subsequent appearance in traffic court; it's church, all of them, all day; it's the liturgy floating in the streets; it's your mama's cassava pie; it's your grandma's cassava pie; it's fishcakes & hot cross buns on Good Friday; it's the kite you made with your uncle, or daddy, or cousin; it's your first patch of road rash; it's the muffler burn on your calf; it's salt water in your hair, pickling your skin, flecking off your eyelashes; it's your ace girl or ace boy; it's hurricane days off from school; it's ducking breeze on pedal bikes; it's jumping off the dock; it's swimming with sneakers on; it's roadside snow balls; it's fried fish from county games; it's the queen's english turned on its head; it's *cha dun, fackin-well, ya mate!*; it's bonfires when the sun sleeps; it's everyday eternal.

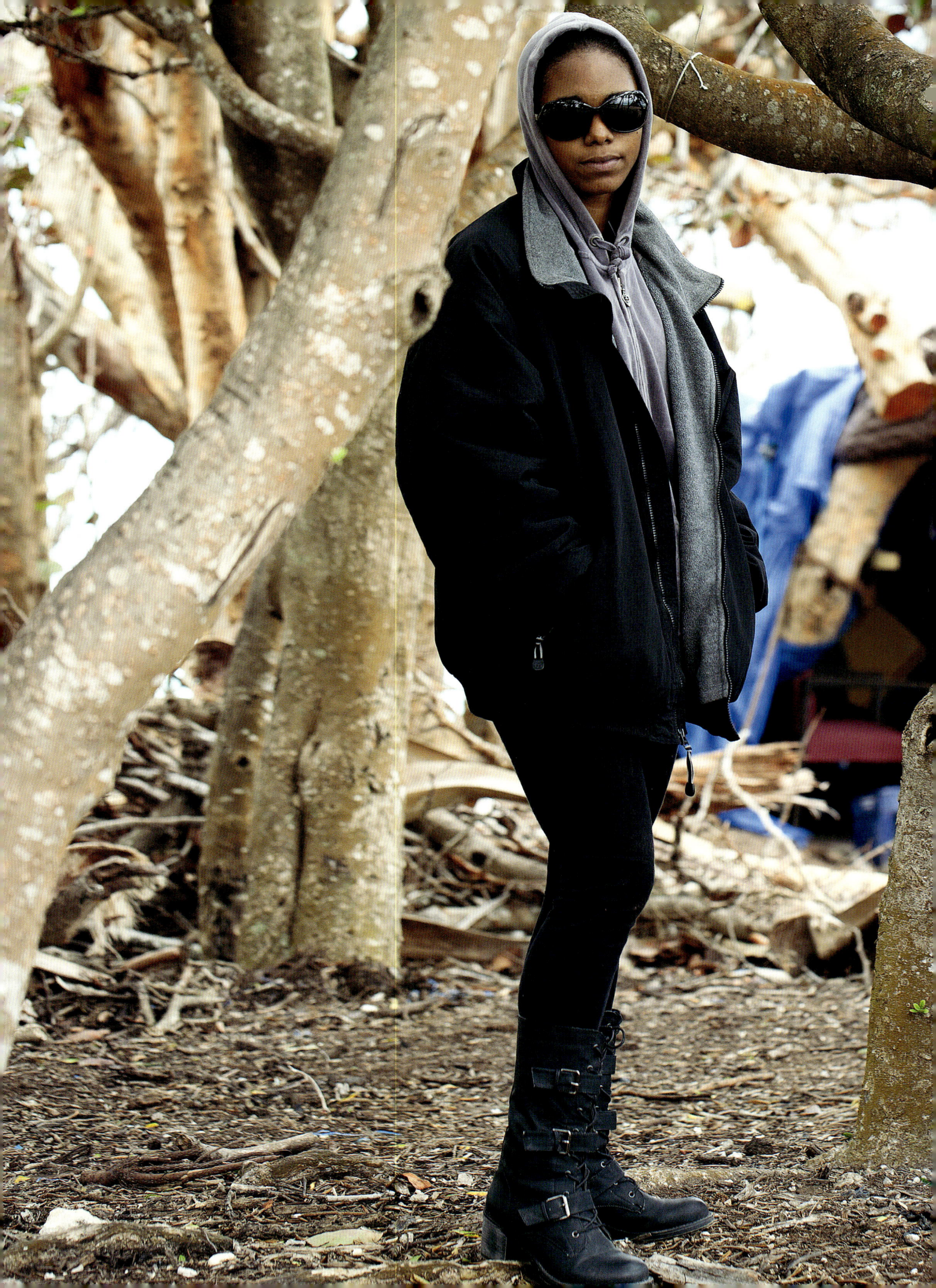

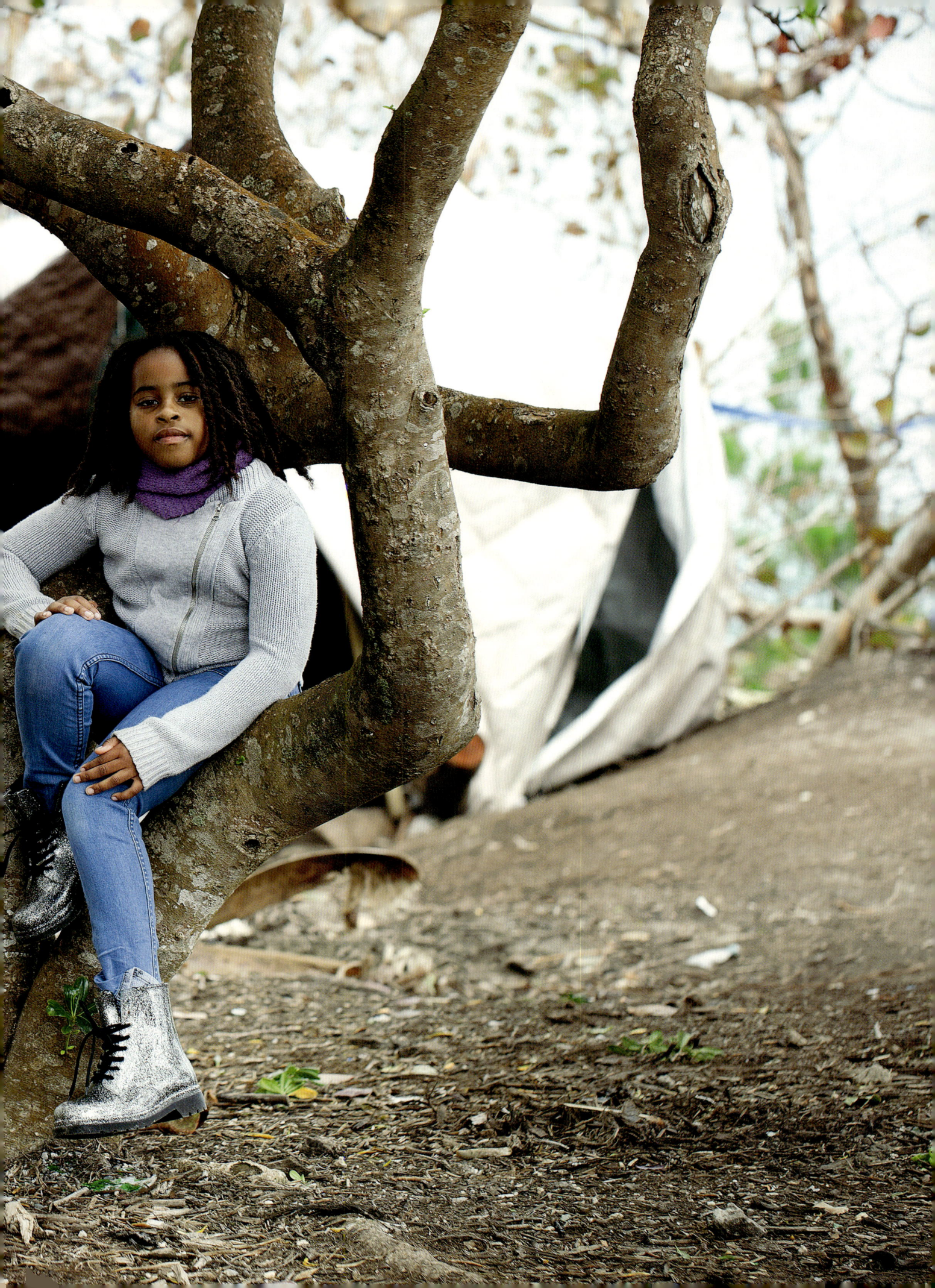

PREVIOUS: *LEAN-TO, NORTH SHORE ROAD, HAMILTON PARISH*

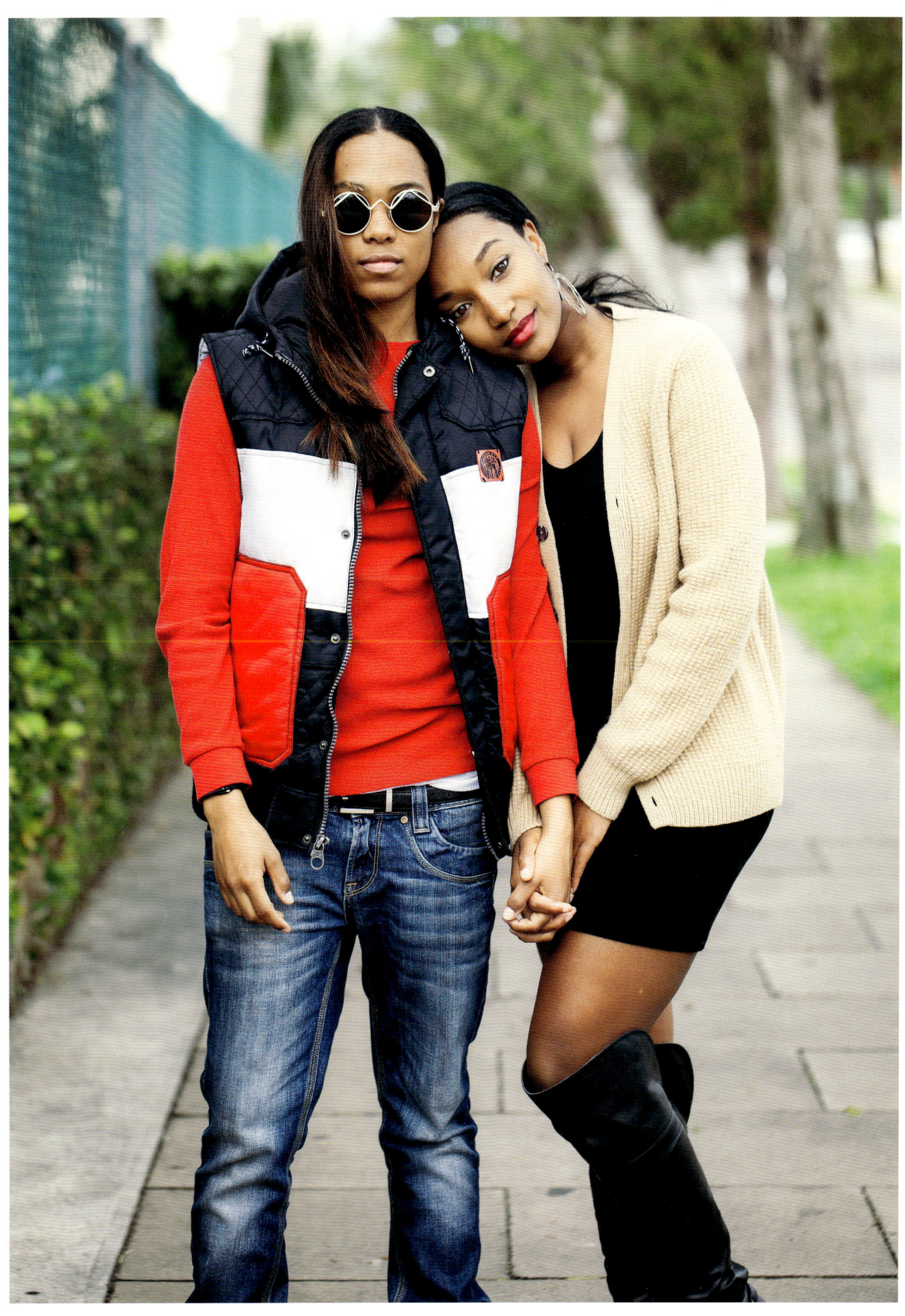

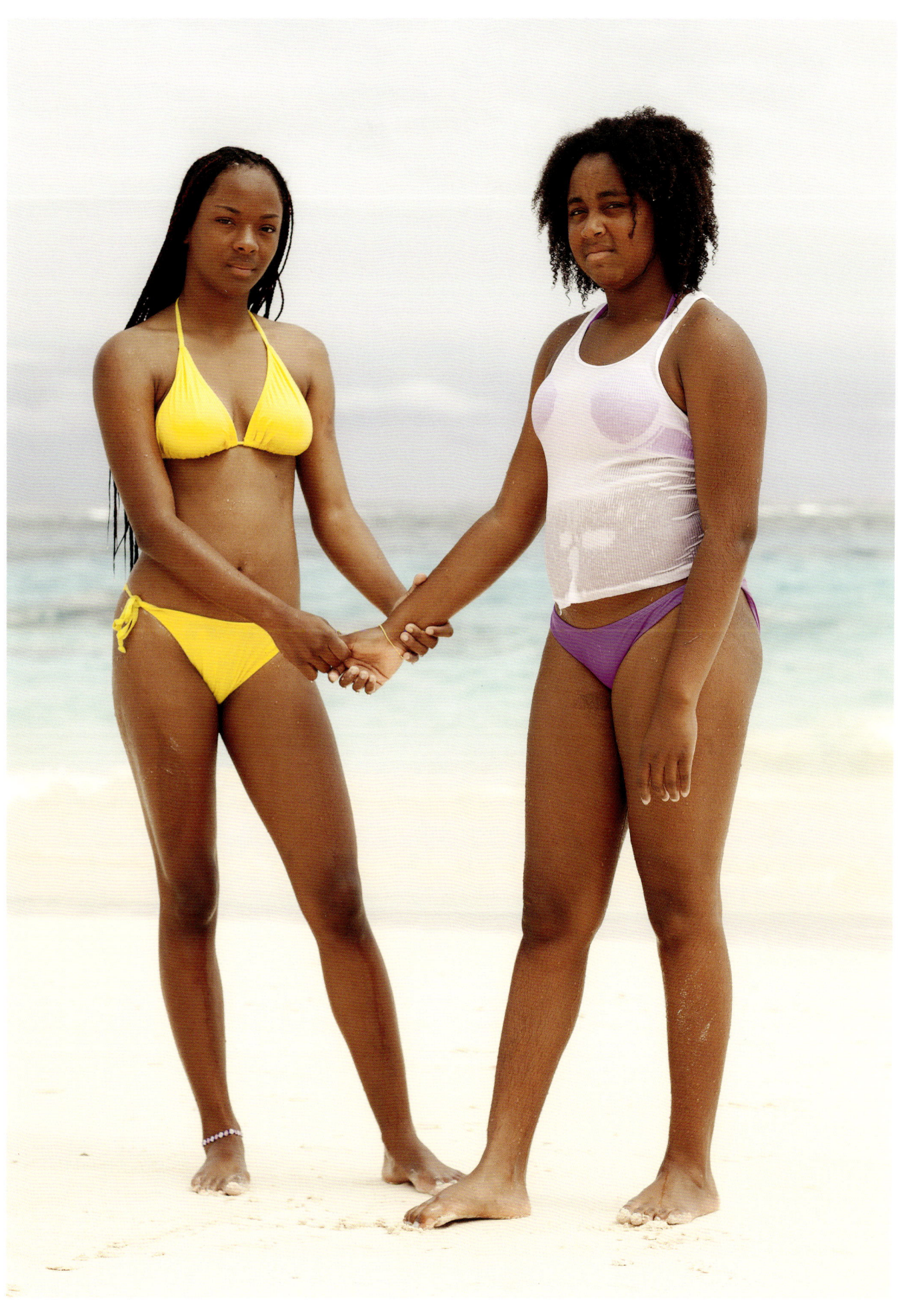

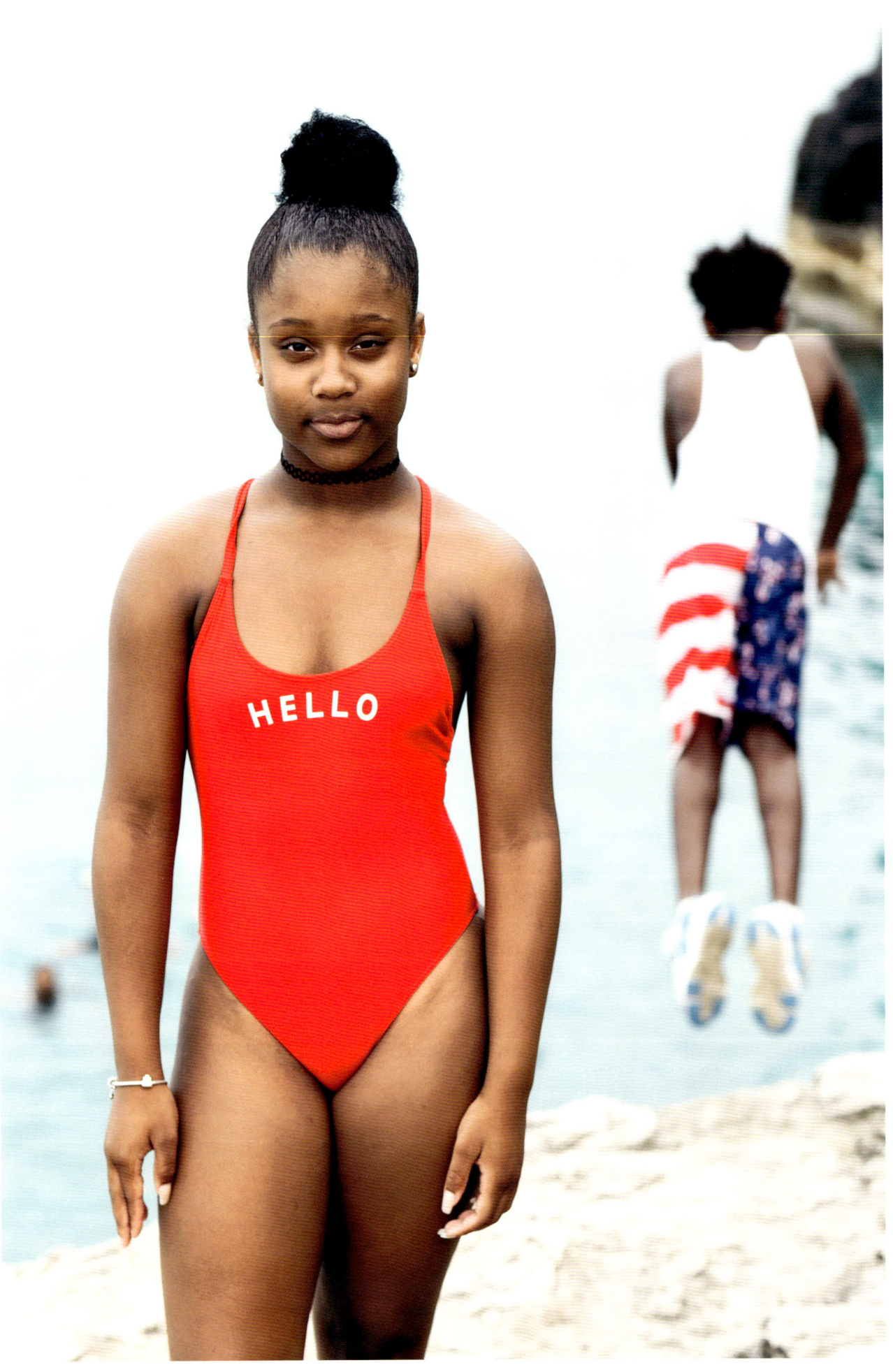

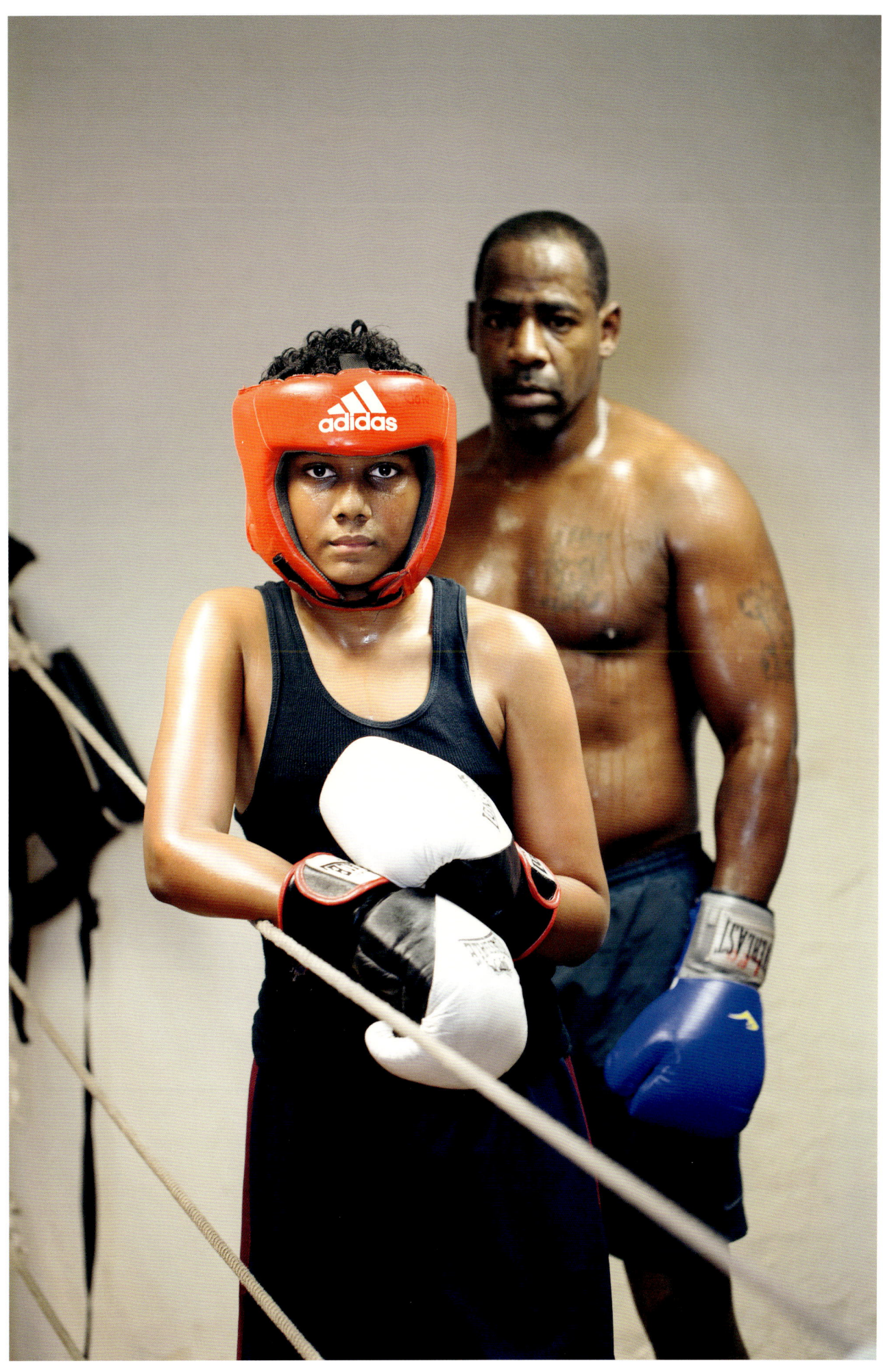

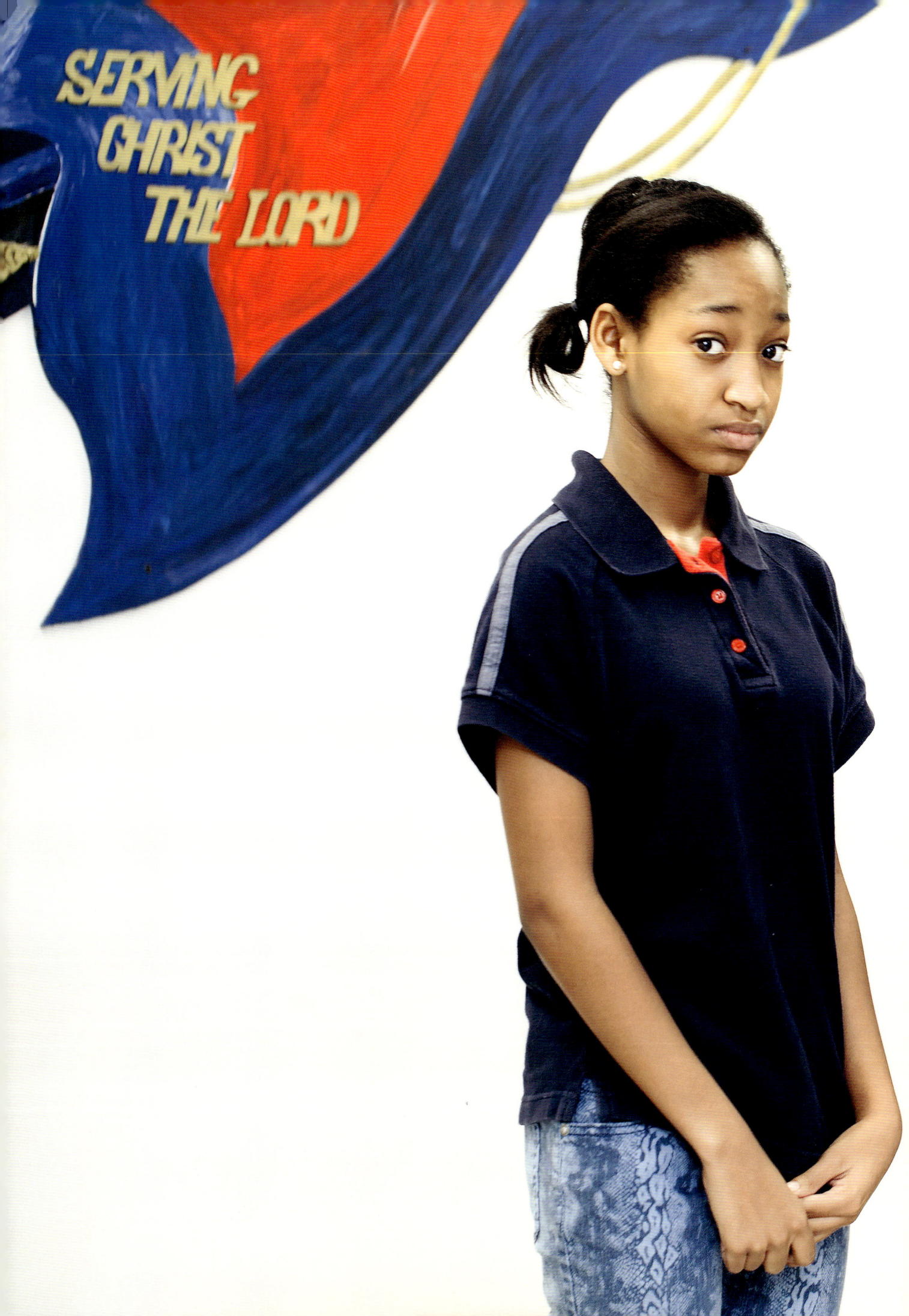

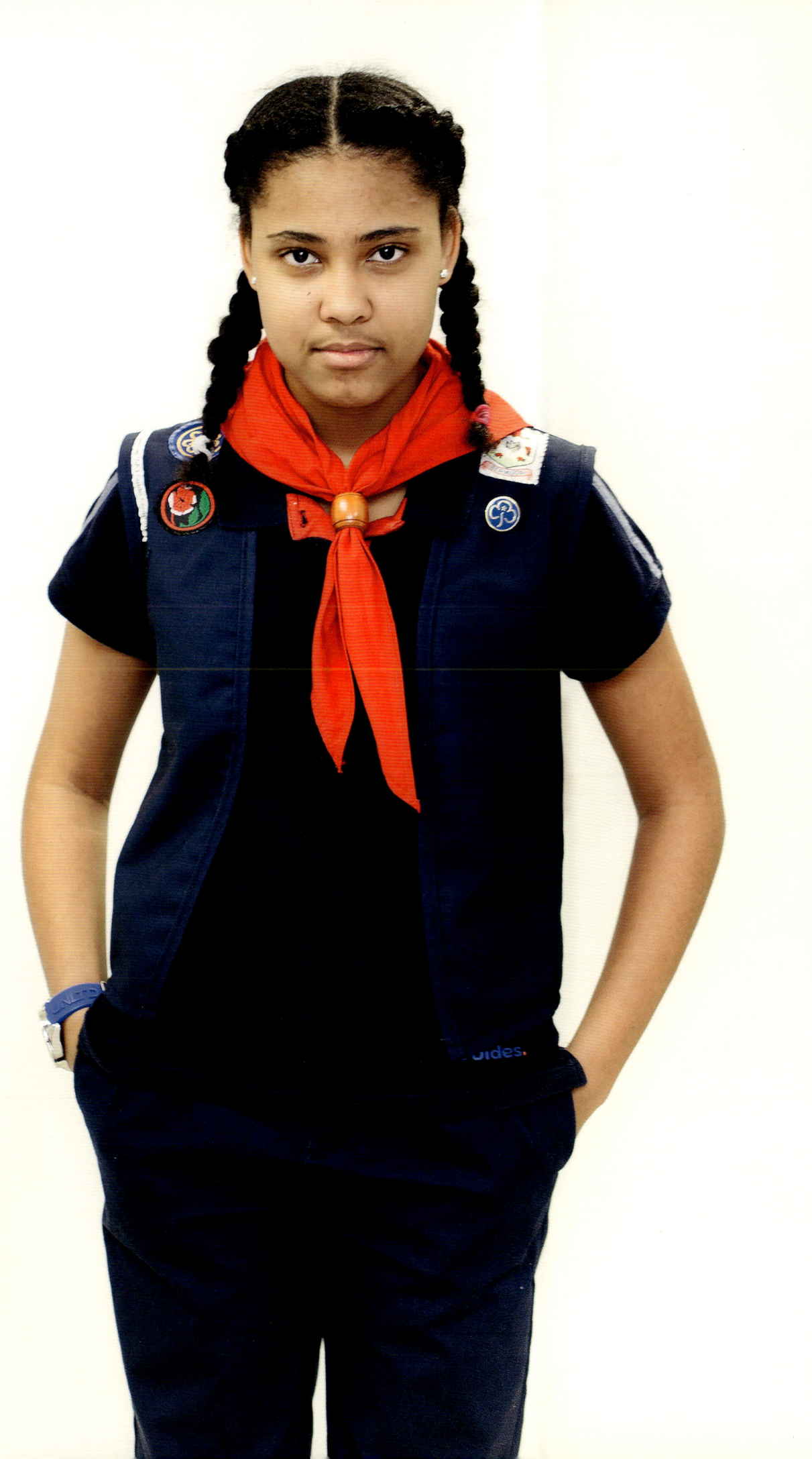

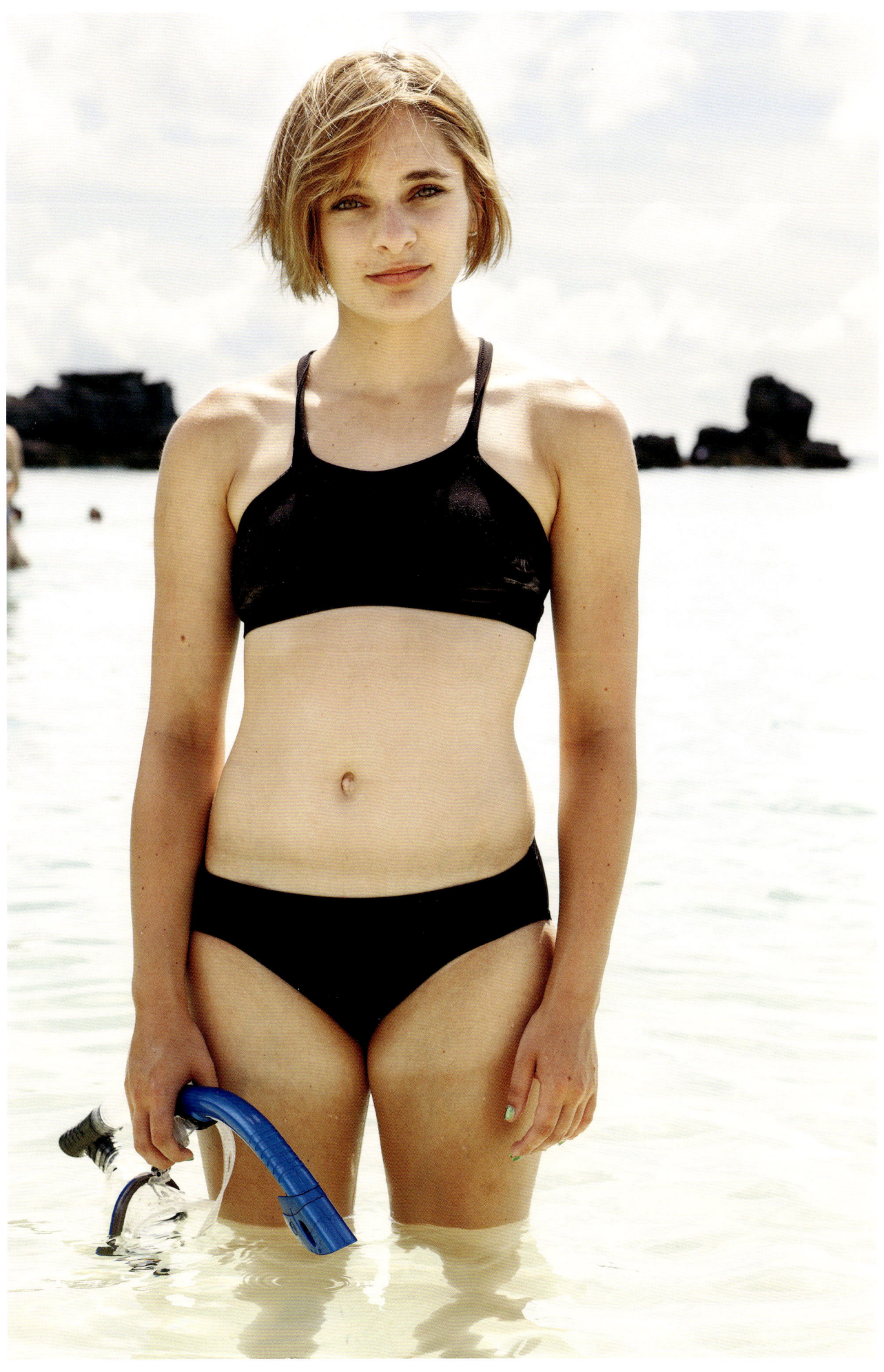

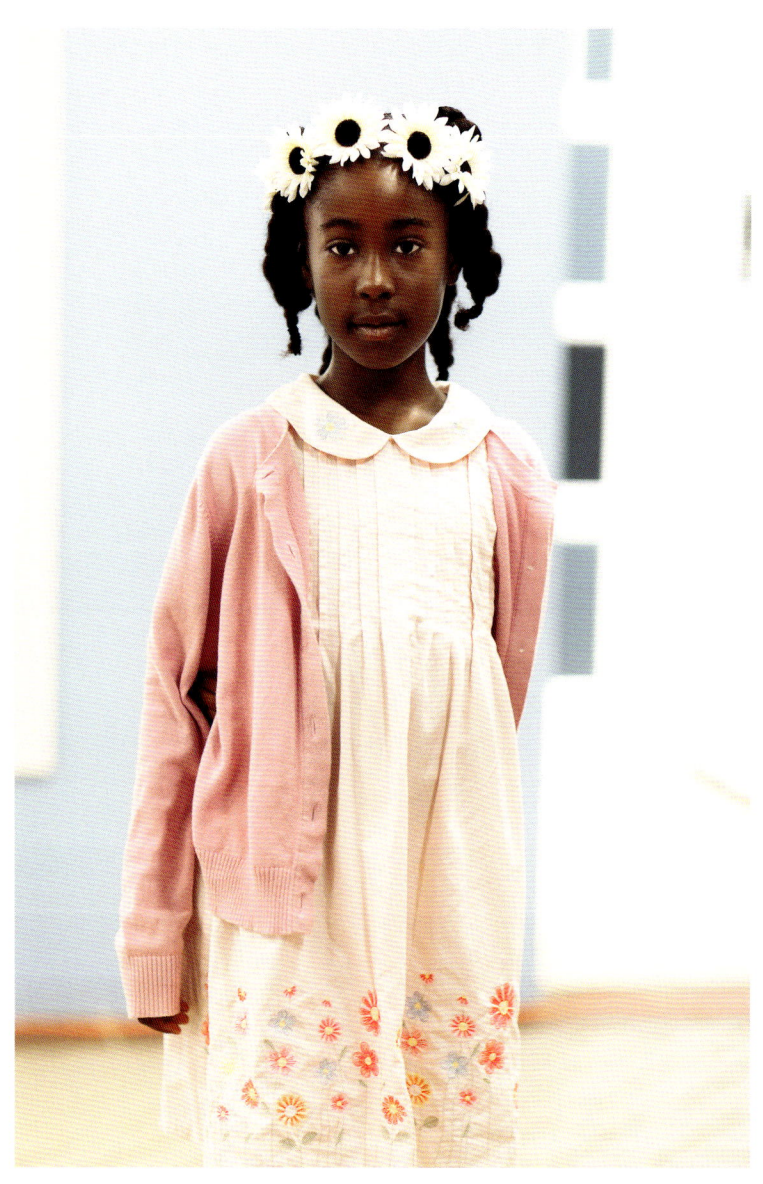

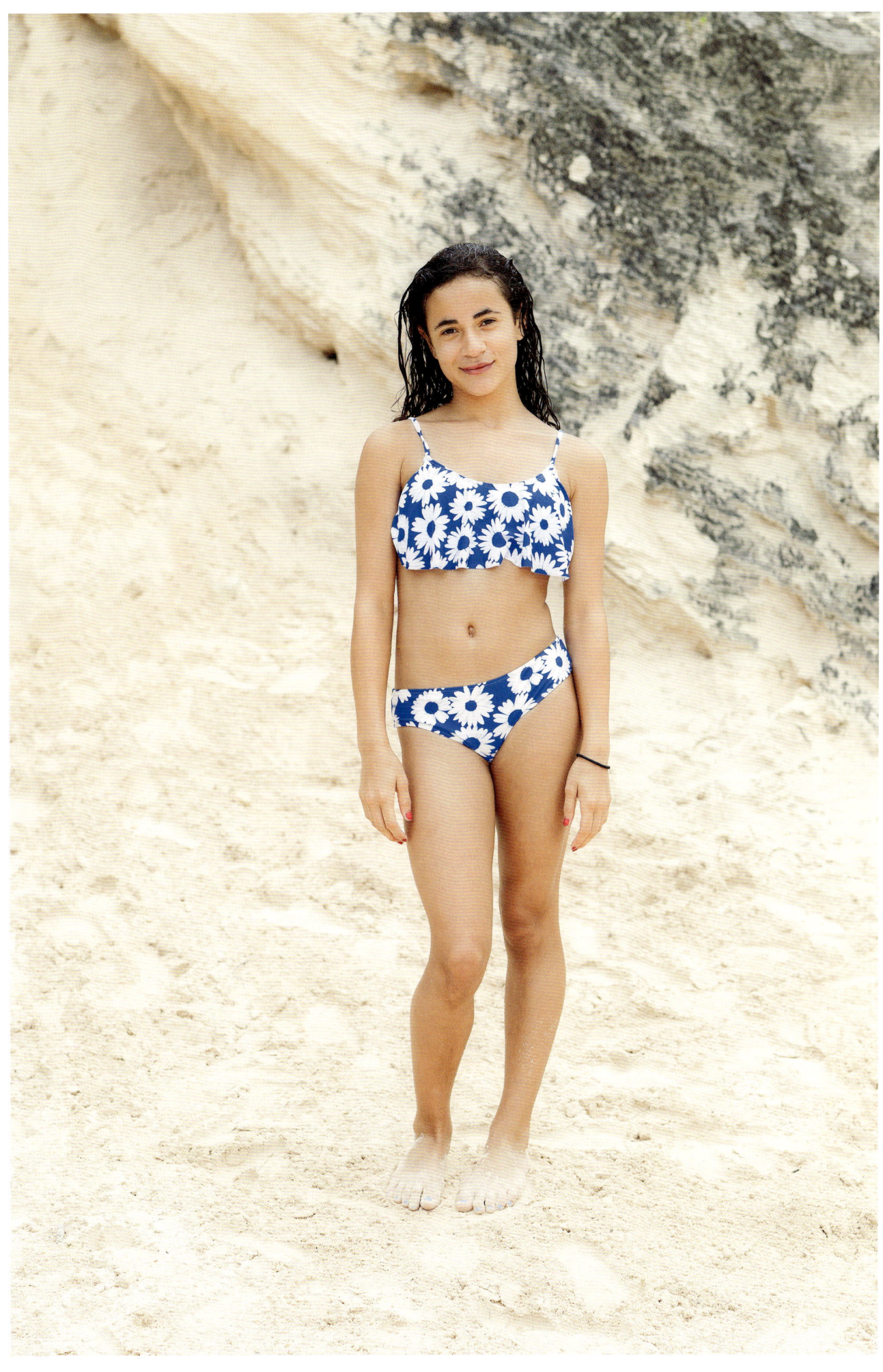

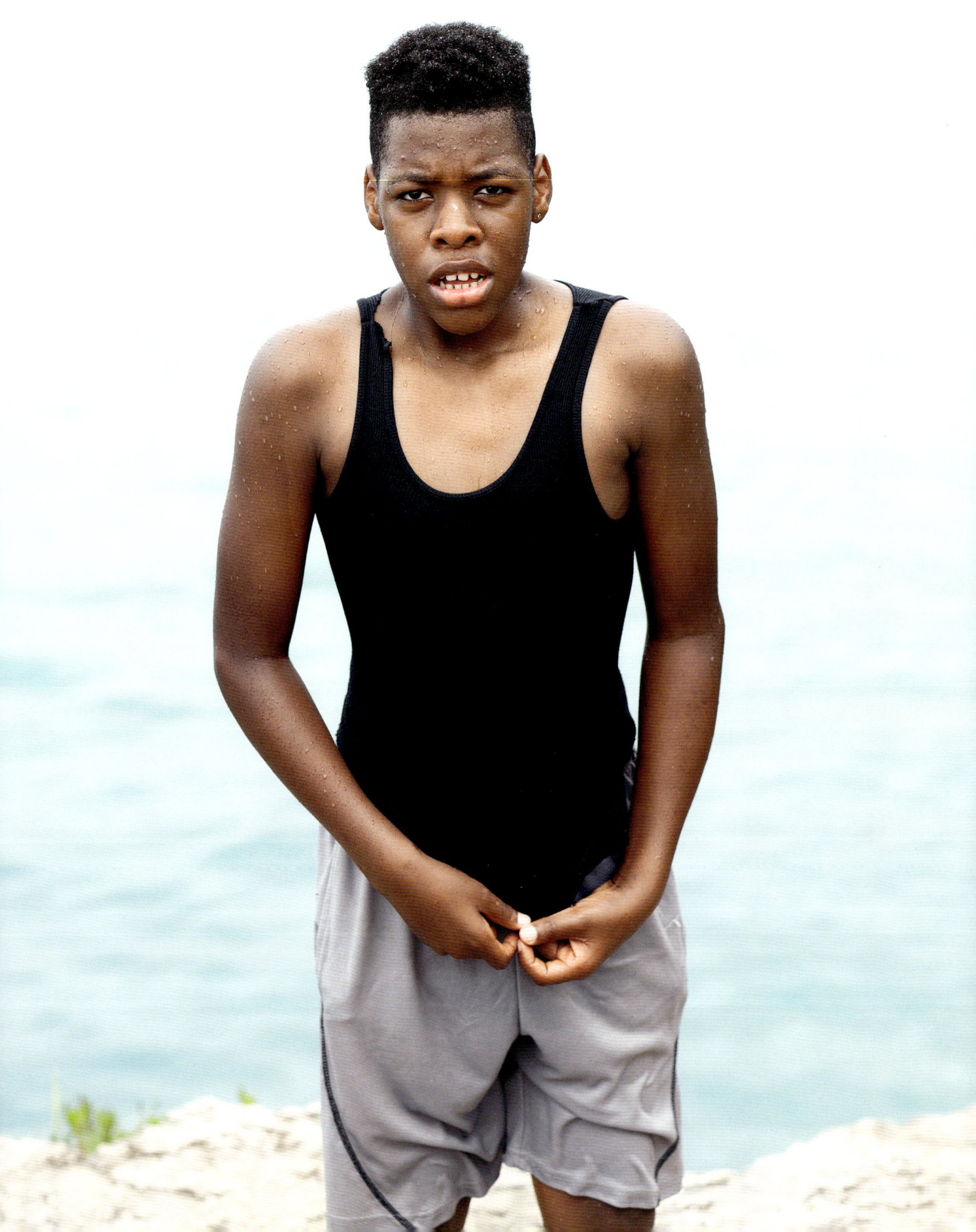

# COMING OF AGE IN WONDERLAND

DEBRA FRIEDMAN

There is something unique about navigating the landscape of "teenagerhood" on an island that is over a thousand kilometers from the nearest landfall. For young people branching out in a hundred directions, there is nowhere to go in a hurry in Bermuda.

Virtually everywhere I went, I found the constituency of teenagers I sought. What struck me most initially was the ubiquitous school uniform consistent with the British influence that still permeates the island. But finally, and the thing that still lingers, ineffably, with me: the matchless way they wore those uniforms (not to mention their lives): awkward, brave, shy and bold, informed by both a sense of style and a genius for beautiful chaos.

The kids I encountered had one foot firmly planted on "The Rock" and the other in their future dreams. Many will go. Some will return. Some will never leave, laying down deep roots right out of high school, nurtured by church, family, and community. But they all will be acutely aware of the difference between "there" and "here," although they may not be able to name it.

One of the essential distinctions of Bermuda over any other place is the light. It is like nothing I have experienced before. It bounces between sky and sea and fills every shadow with an open-ended brilliance. Eyes appear brighter, skin more luminous. But if it provides an ideal illumination for pictures, it also serves as a guiding metaphor for this project. With light opening every shadow, it is hard to hide with your secrets. This island is an open book. And teenagers need their secrets. If Wonderland sounds a little like the paradise that Bermuda is, it also recalls Alice's free fall down the rabbit hole. The land of teenage is free and fraught, dark and light, euphoric and fearful.

Making a portrait is a collaboration between subject and sitter. To create a portrait is to balance a manipulation of the sitting with the subject's instinct to present himself or herself in a certain way. If you're lucky, the push and pull of that struggle will reveal a small window of truth. Within the sameness of a uniform, whether government issue or fashion convention, I rely on the smallest detail of costume, gesture, expression, or pose to reveal everything. It is in peering through that small opening in the emotionally perilous landscape these kids traverse, engaged in the act of "becoming," that the picture lies.

It is often such a small detail that draws me to a subject. A detail that is easy to miss but tells me everything I need to know about the individual I am photographing. A schoolgirl in her uniform is completely disheveled when she stops for me after school and gives me permission to photograph her. Against a grocery store wall she places a fist on her hip and gazes at me directly, confidently. Her eyes are beautiful, clear, and hazel. But for me it's the bobby pins lined up at the ready that sit displayed on her jacket pocket, ready to bring some order to the chaos of her presentation, her wild hair. Chaos and order are always at battle in the land of teenage.

For some, order is everything. The perfectly pressed uniform. The prefect and best-girl badges sewn carefully and just so. A girl stands for me with her legs crossed where she is planted. It's the badges. It's the crossed legs. It's the wind that blows her hair out of perfect place. This portrait becomes about control and perfection whether or not it is true for this girl. Another day, a beautiful young boy stands in the school yard, where I encounter him. He is holding a leaf in his fingers. Here, for me, it is simply the leaf in his delicate grasp.

What underlies these pictures and what resonates for me in familiar ways is the eloquent uncertainty of teenagers. There is a vitality to this time of life, when you are as self-possessed and full of bravado as you are achingly wedded to "the tyranny of cool." Young people share a desire to fit in that often works at cross-purposes with their need to be distinct. Isn't this at the core of being teenage? All of us will live it, and inevitably remember it. It is my deepest hope that the photographs I have created in Bermuda present these particular teenagers as the indelible icons that they are—each and every one.

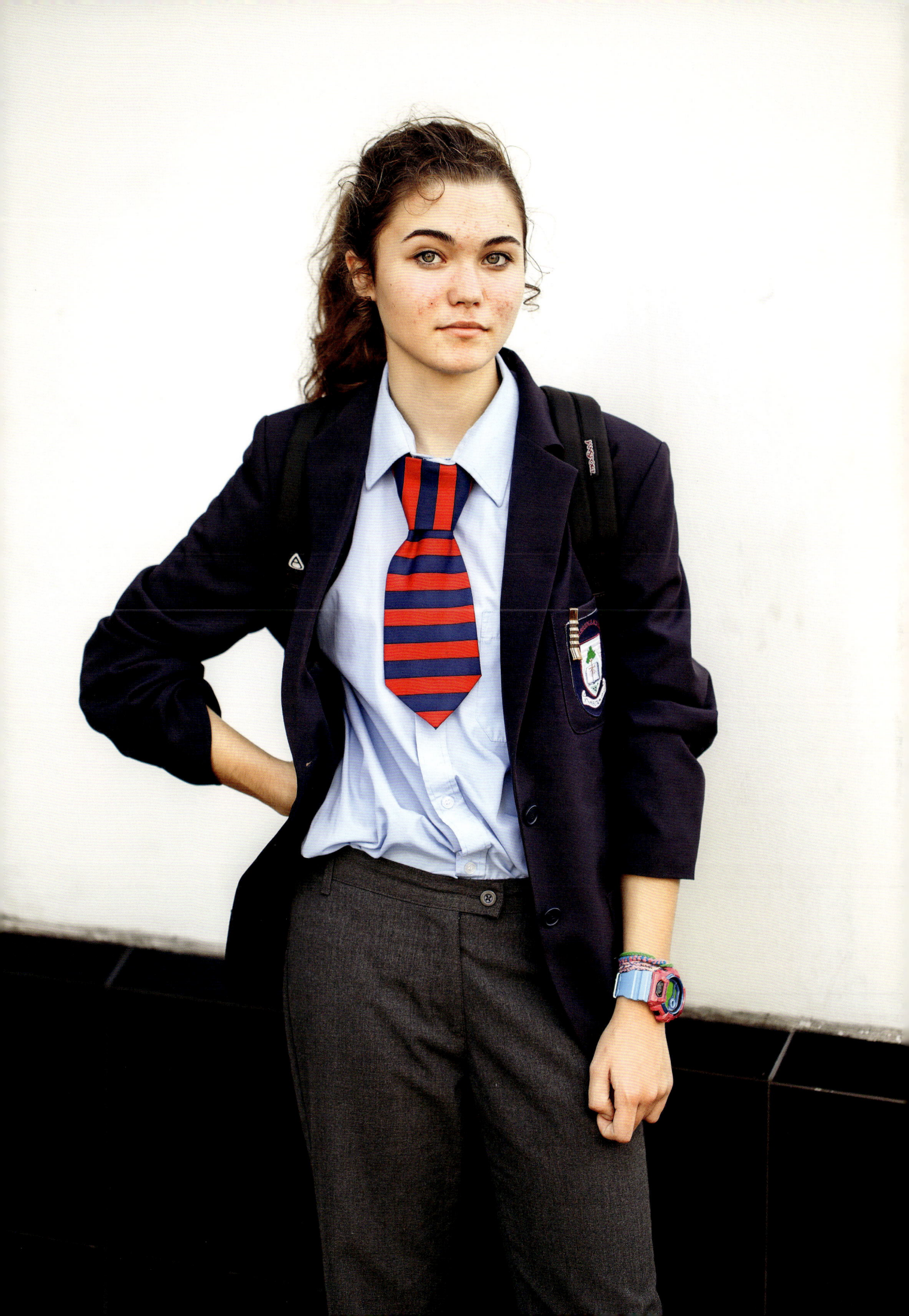

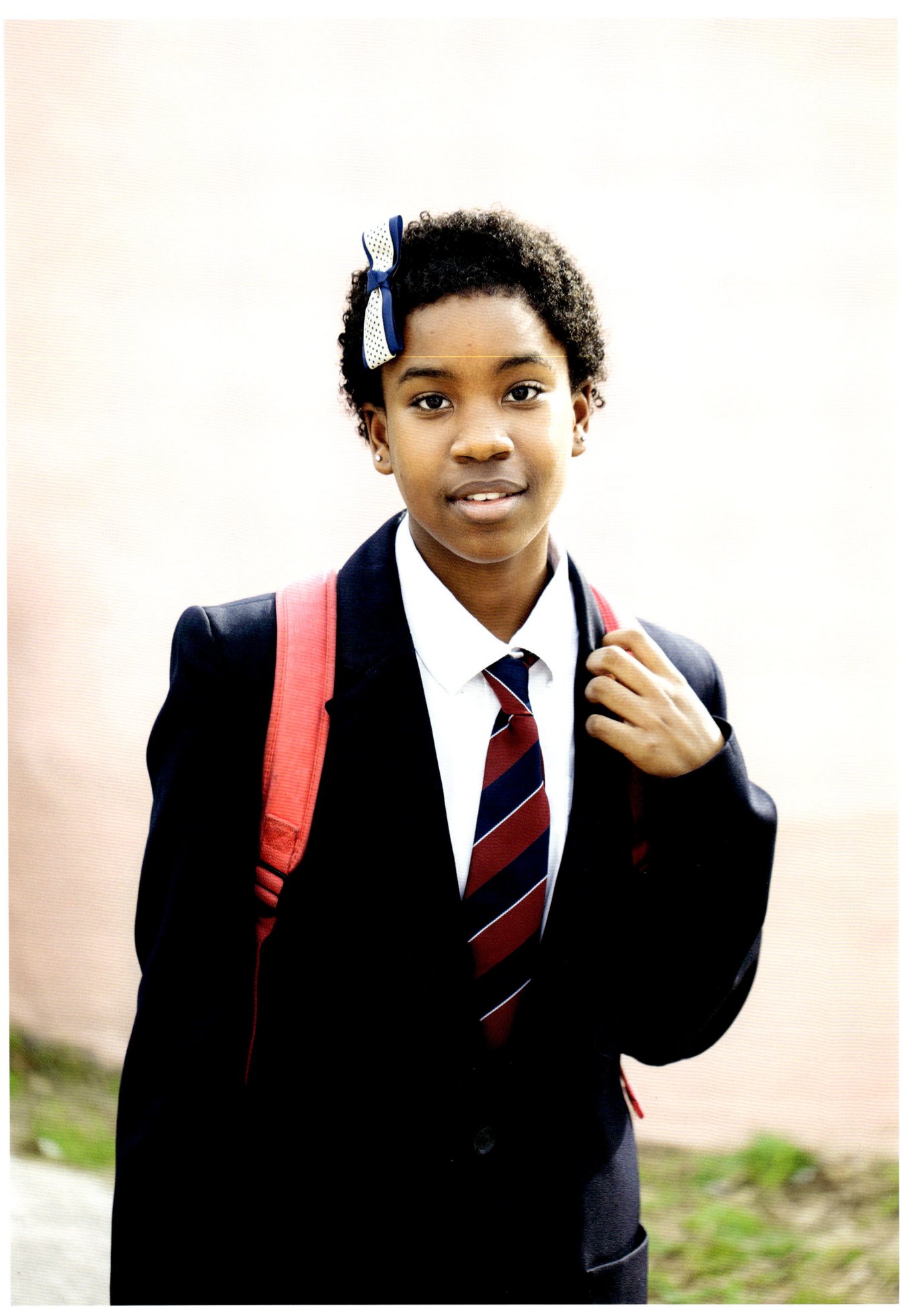

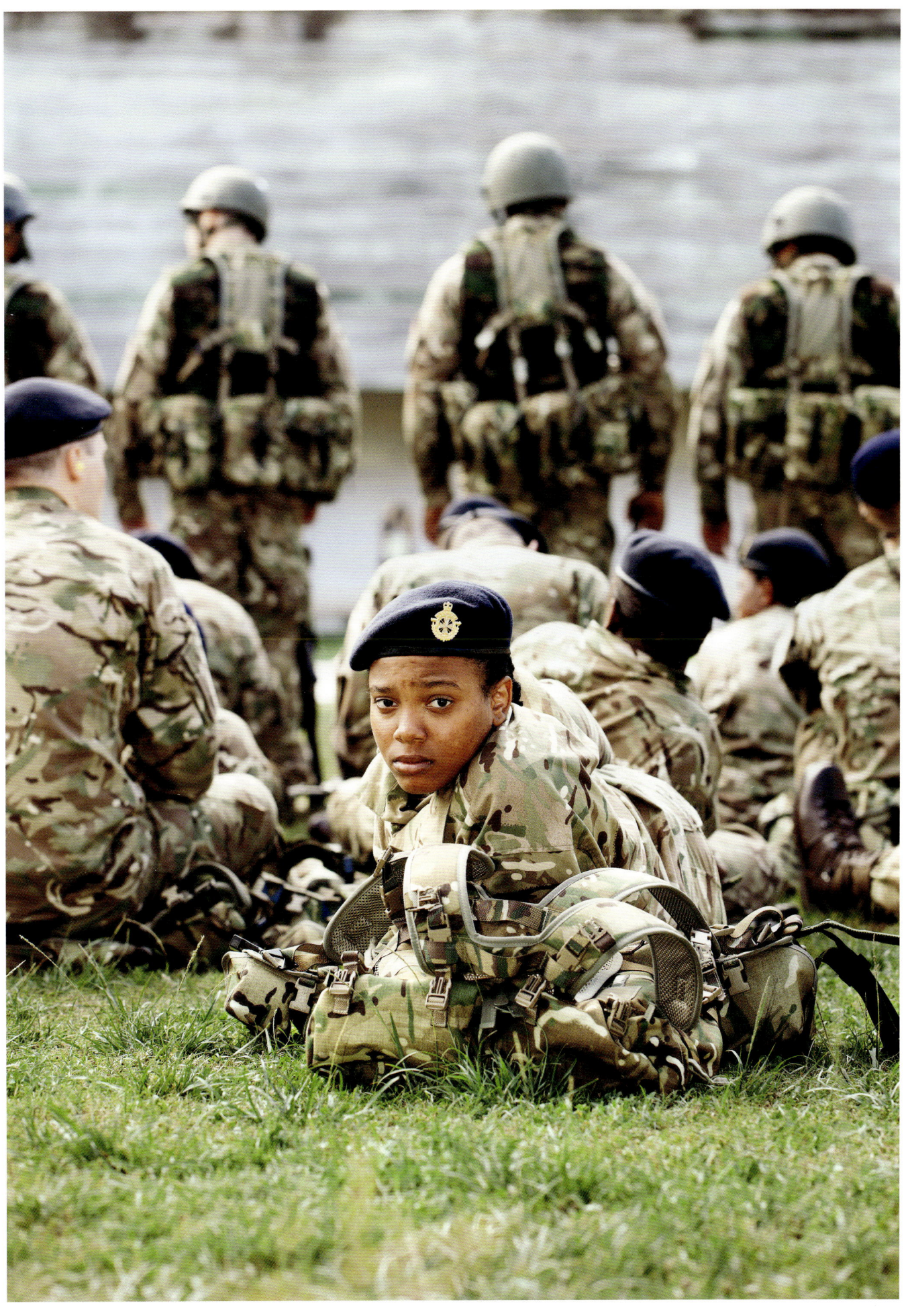

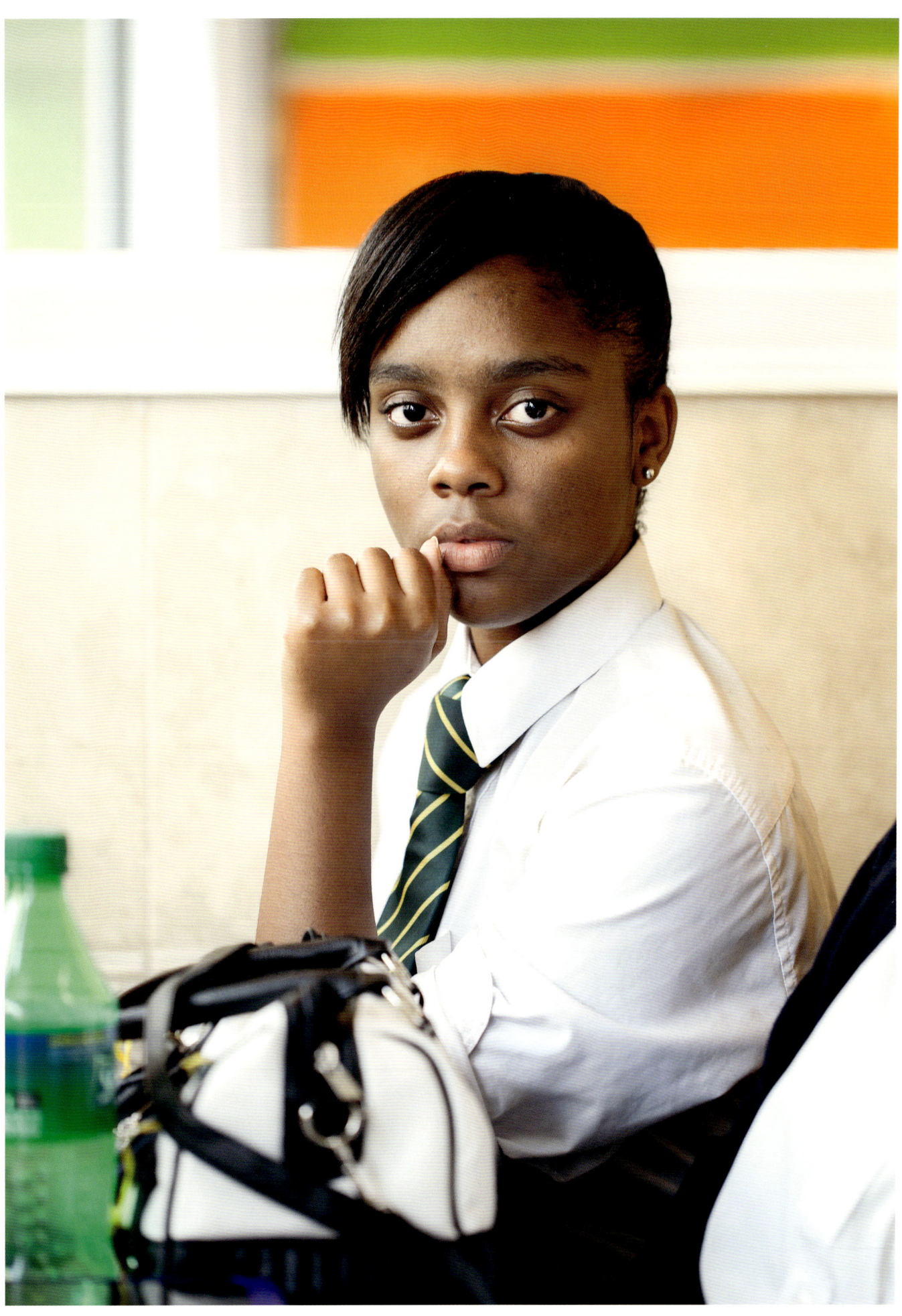

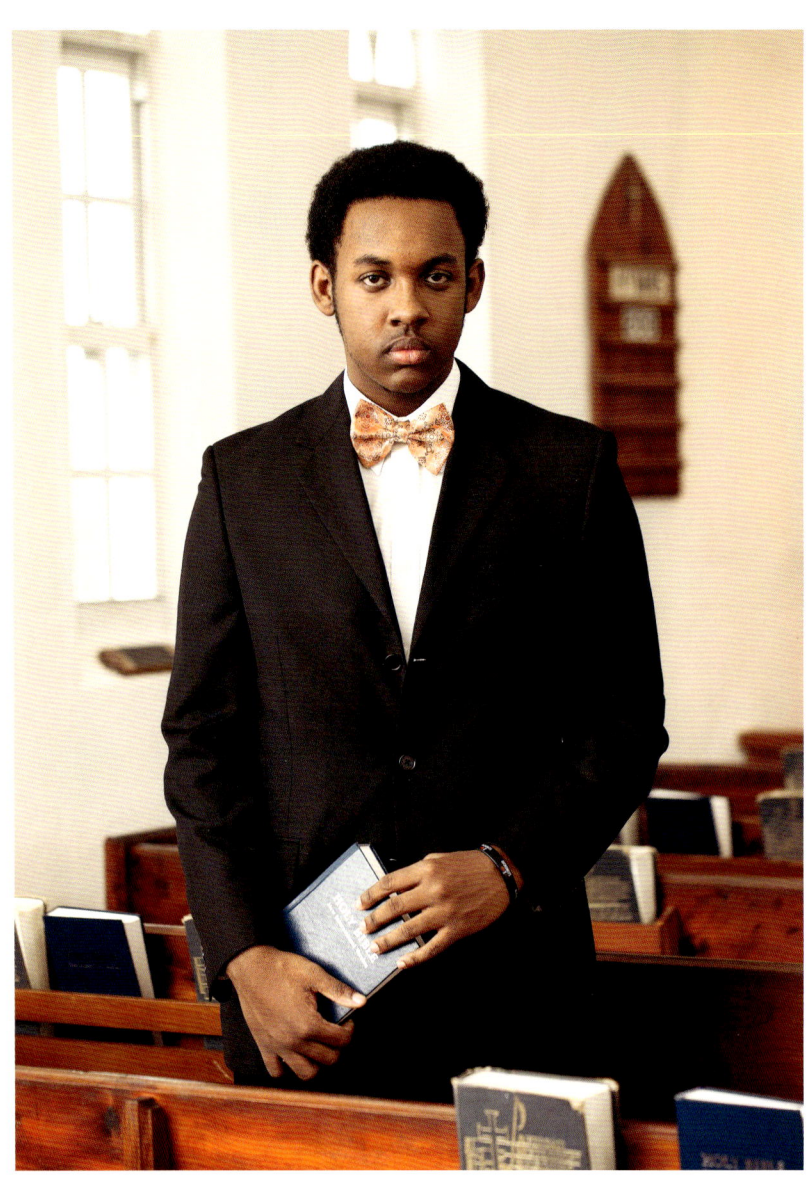

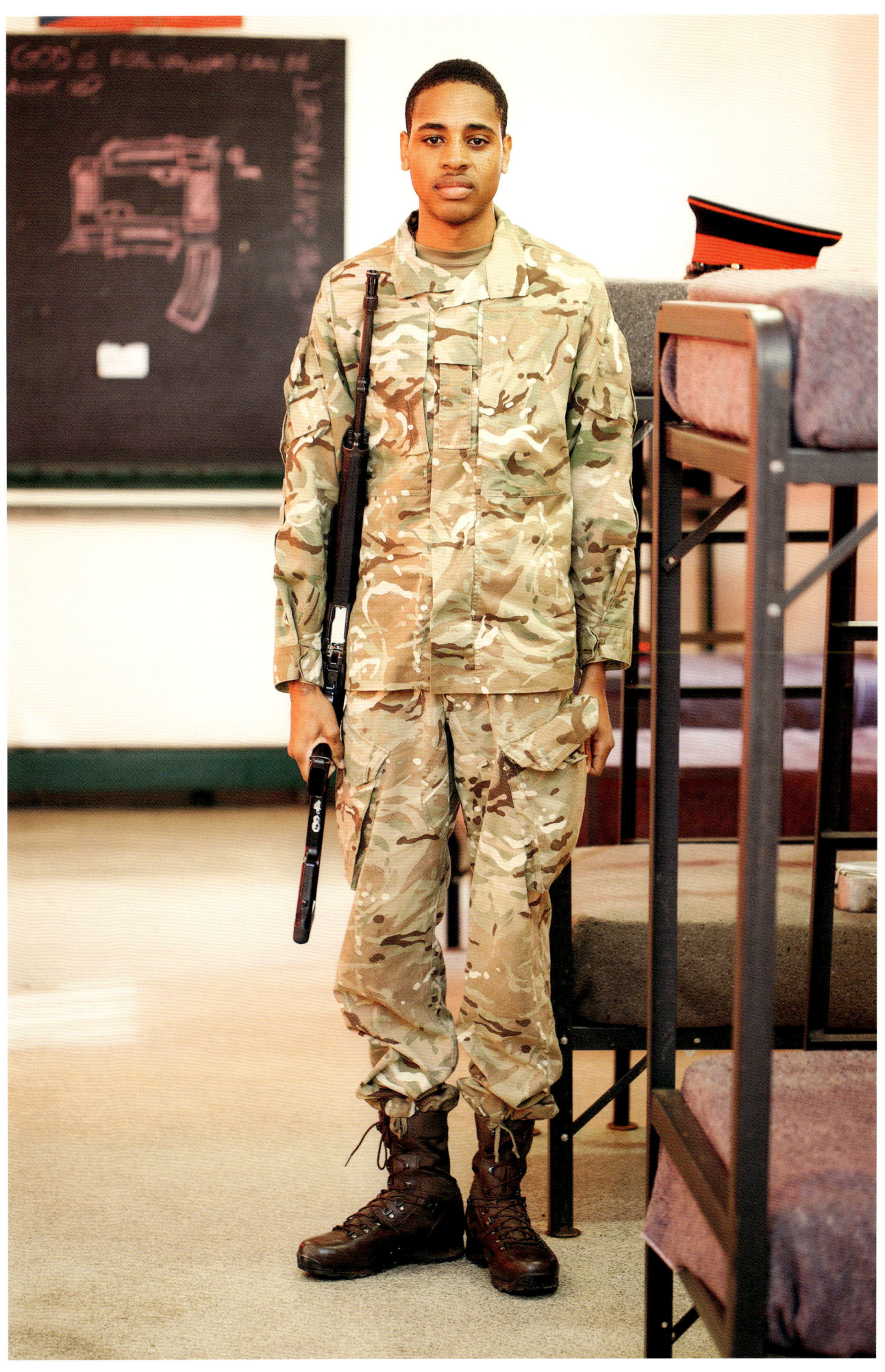

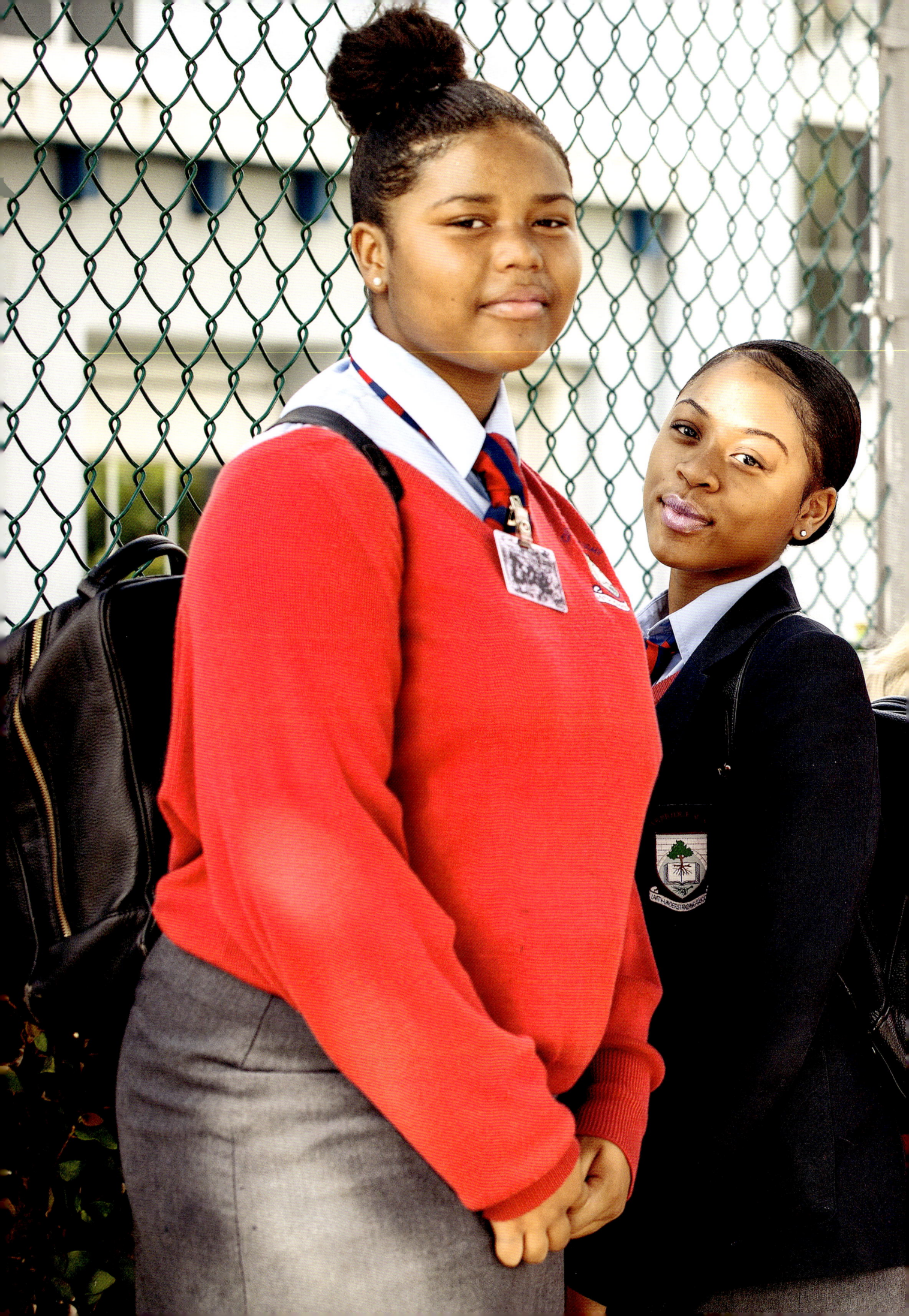

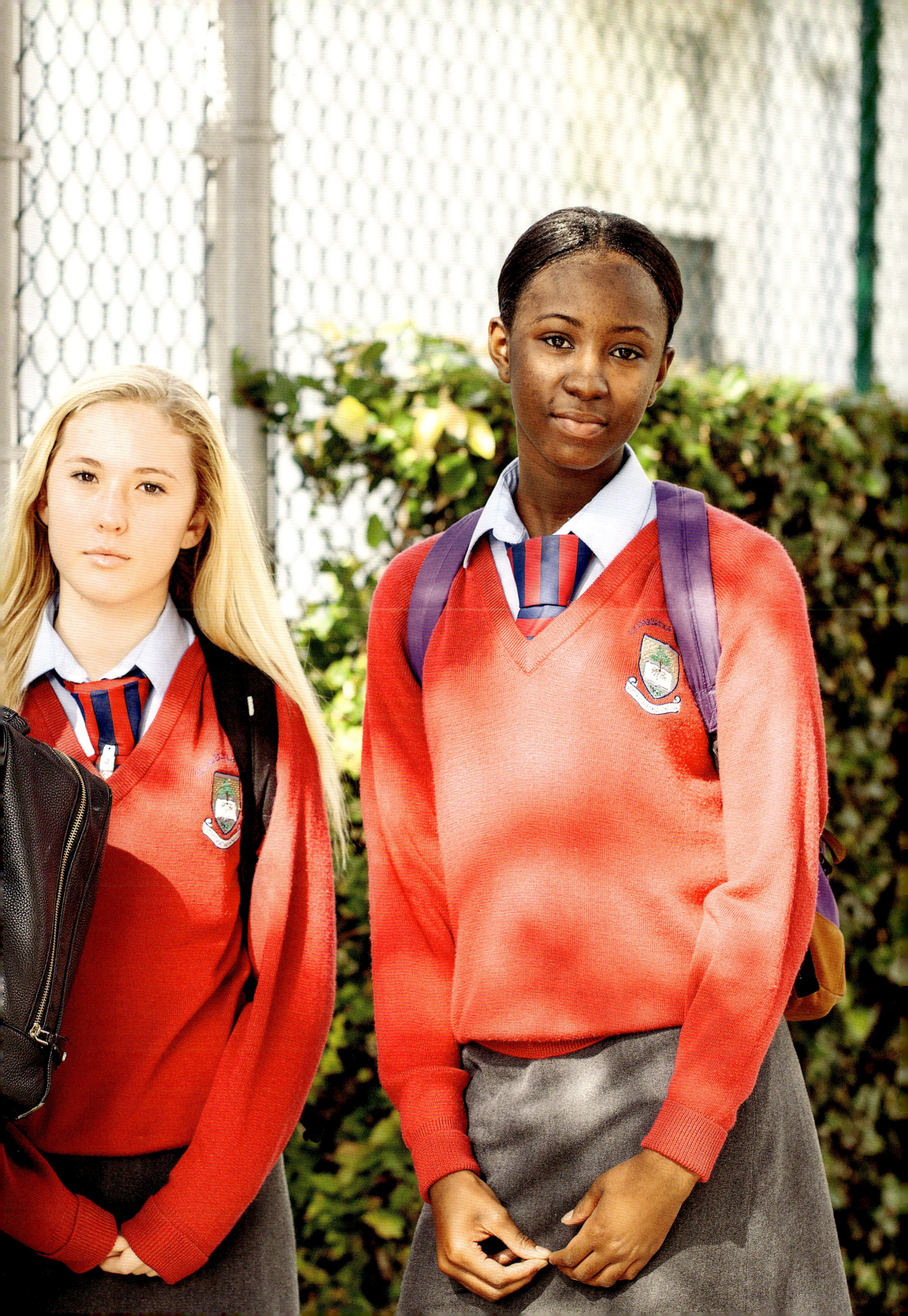

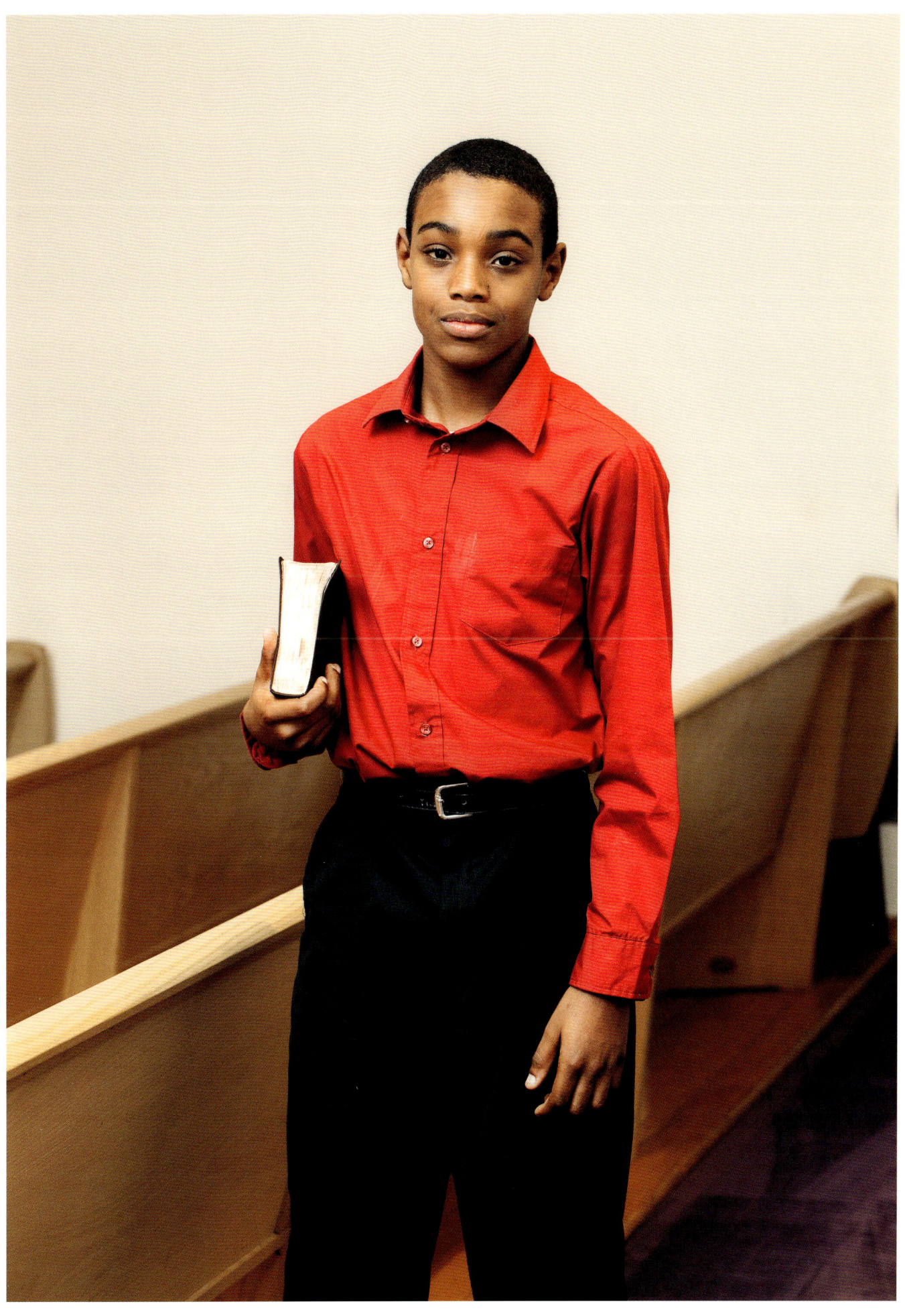

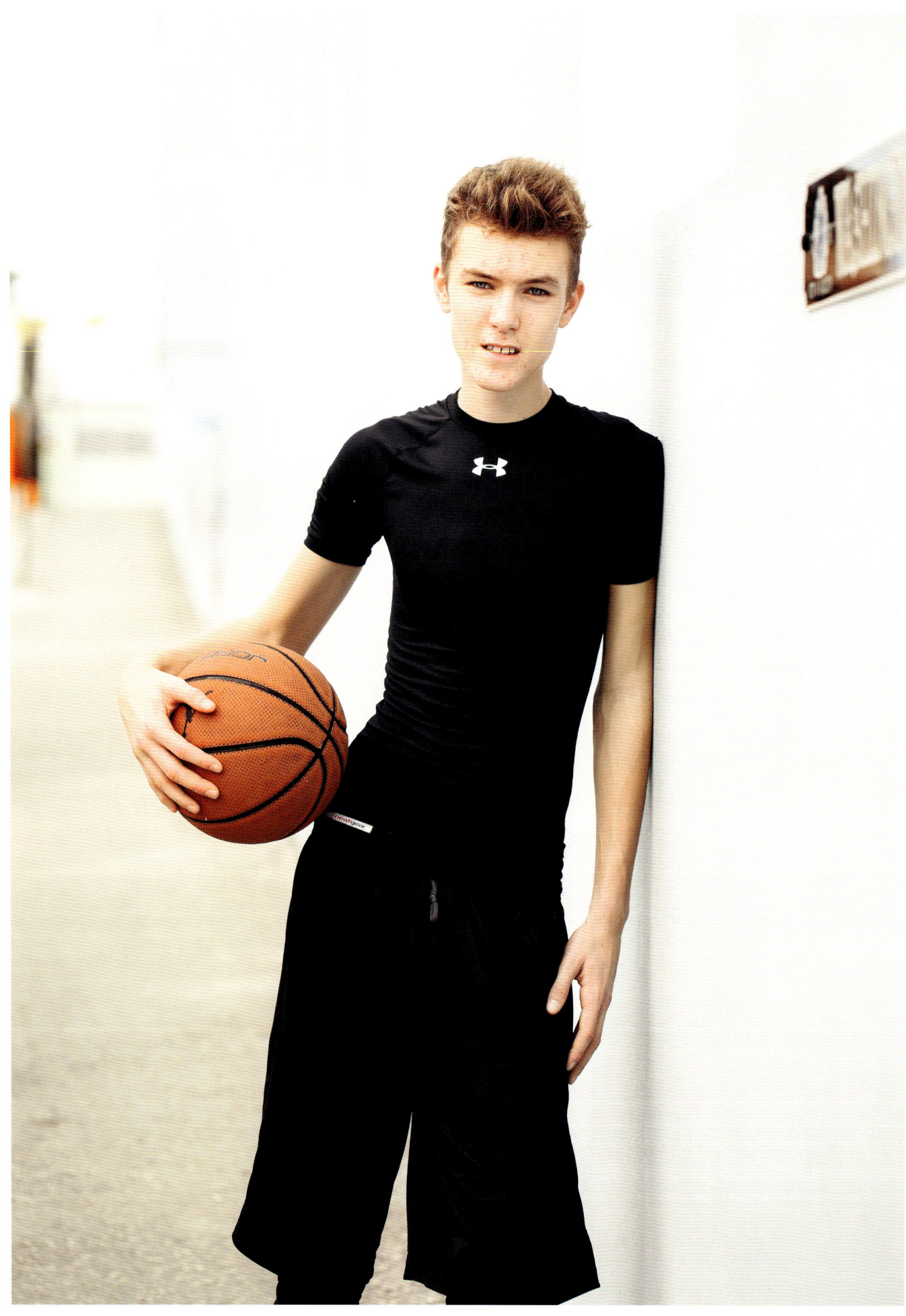

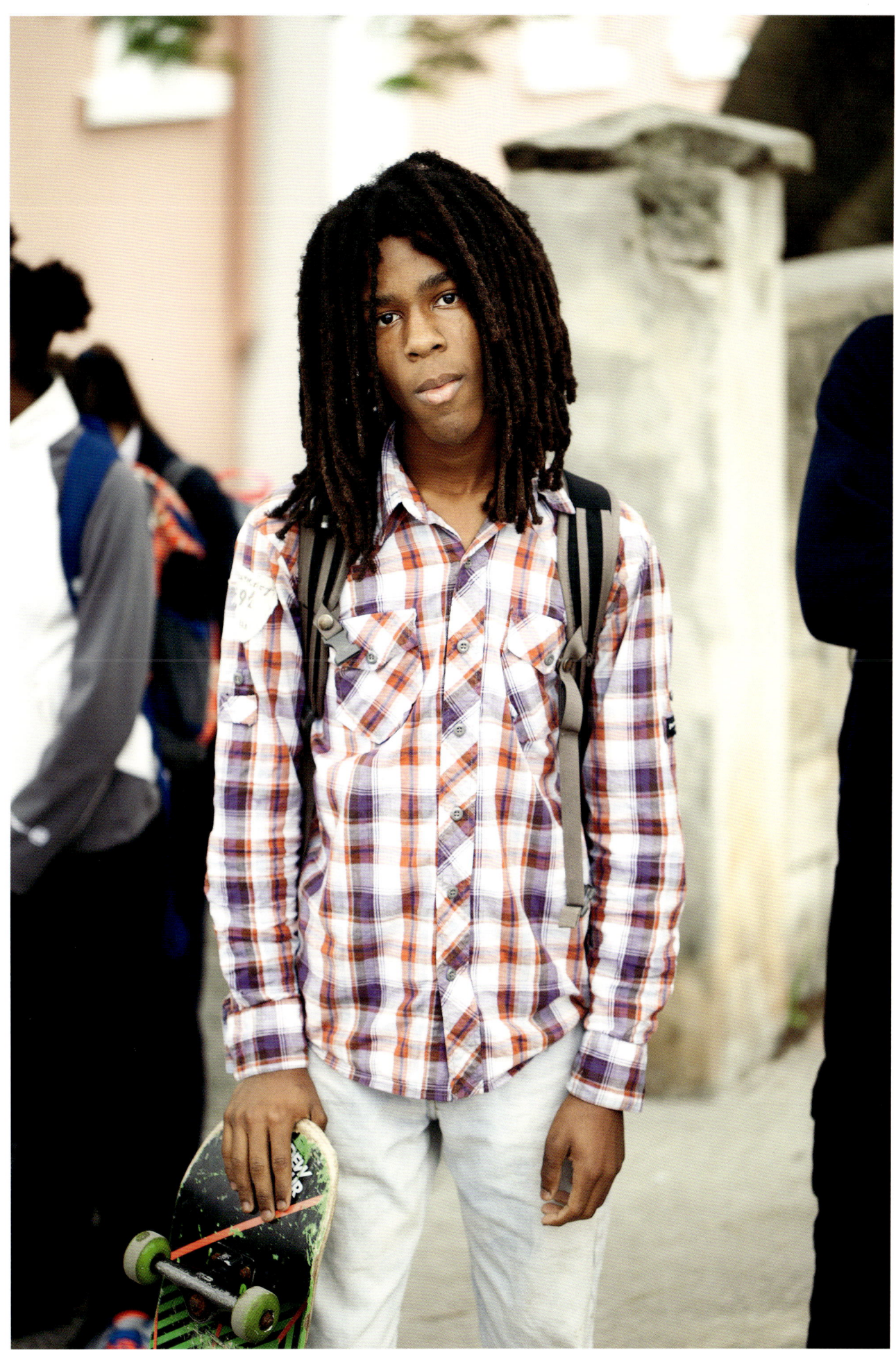

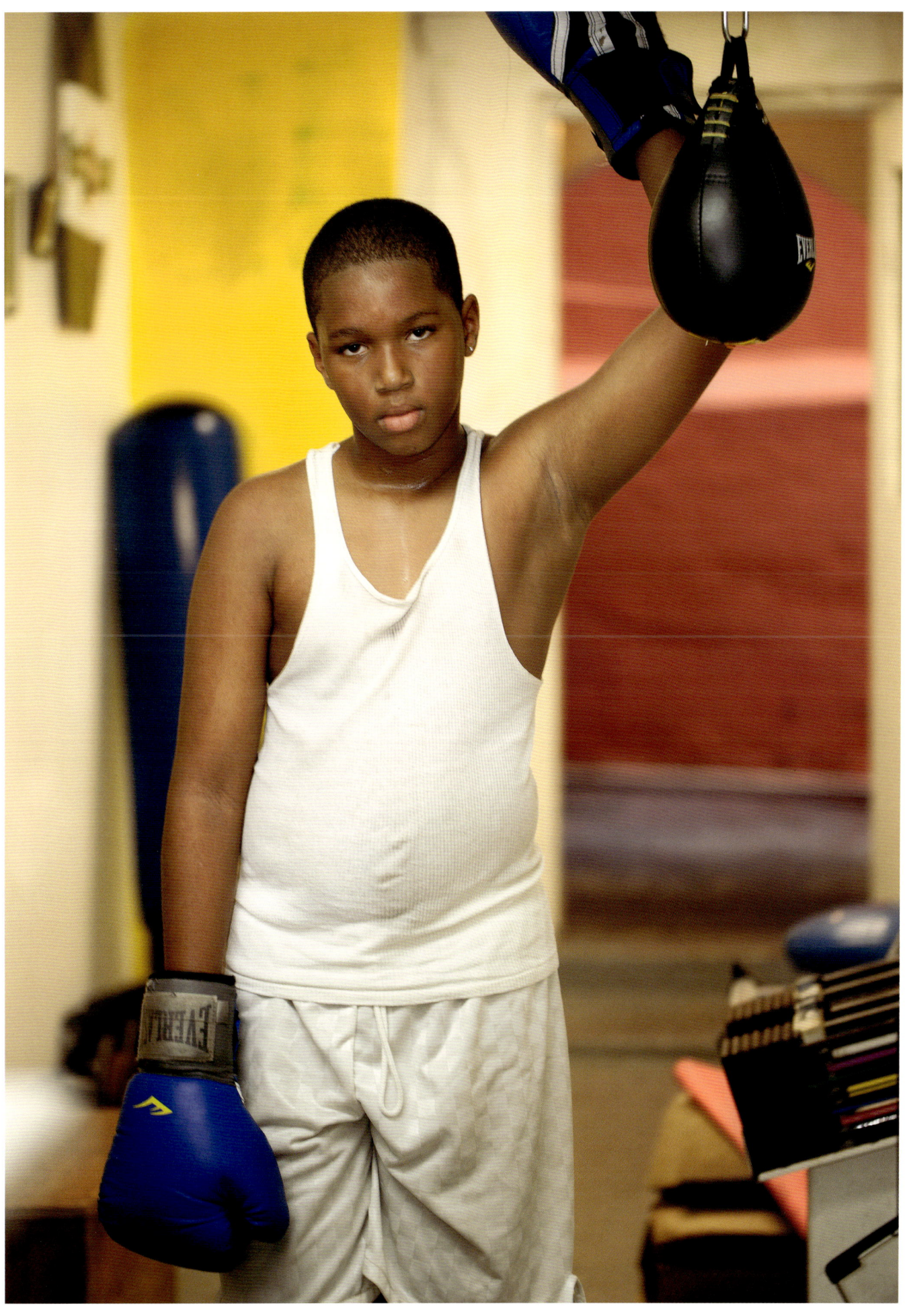

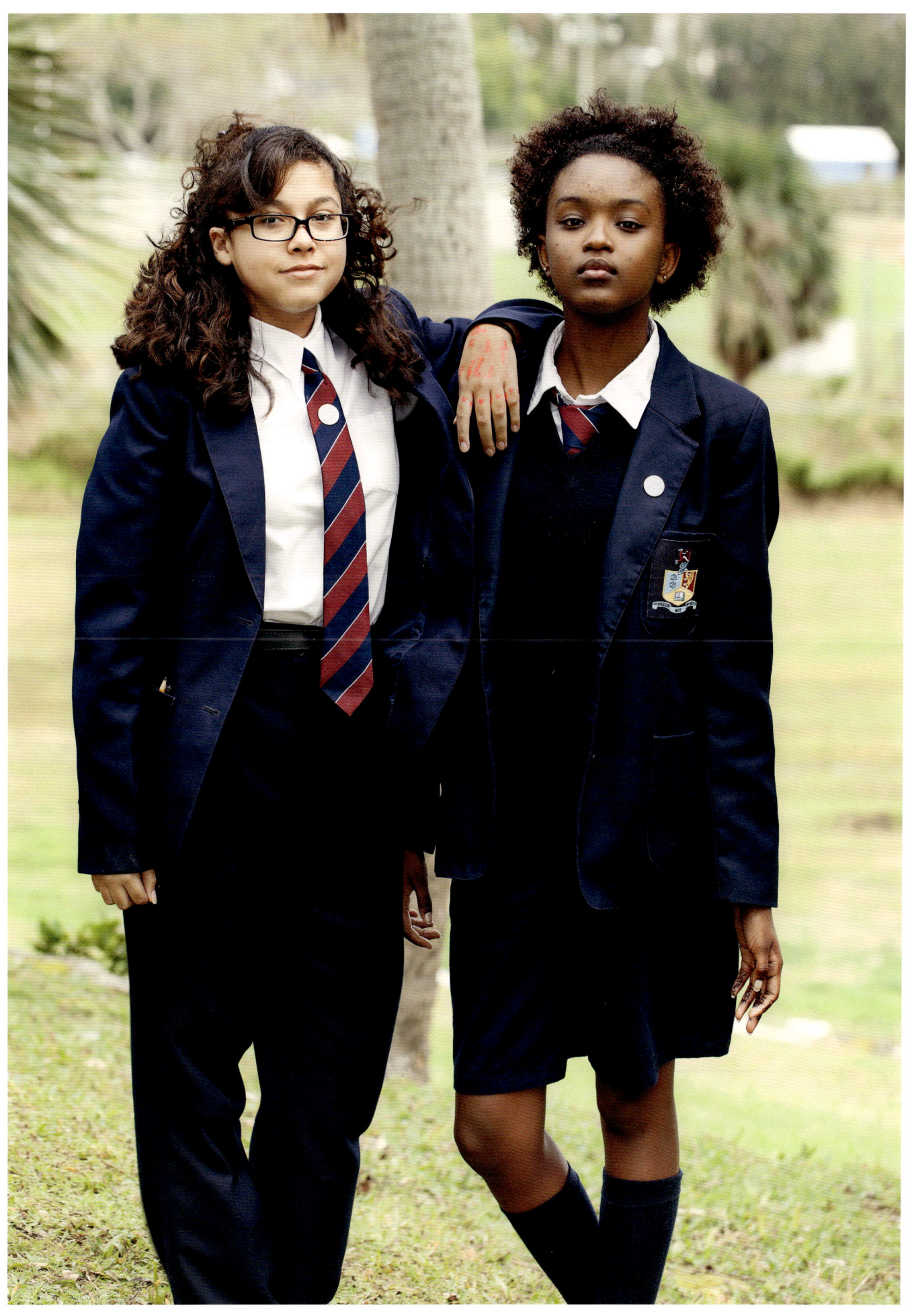

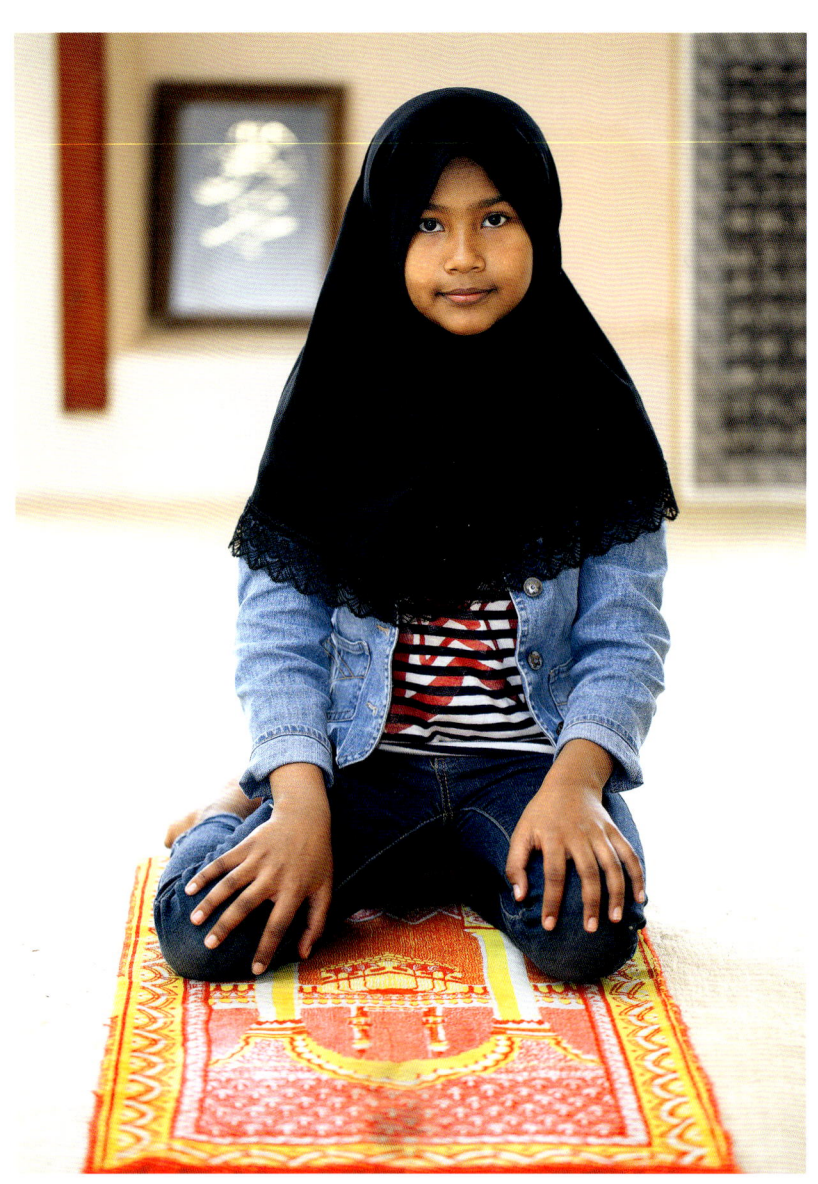

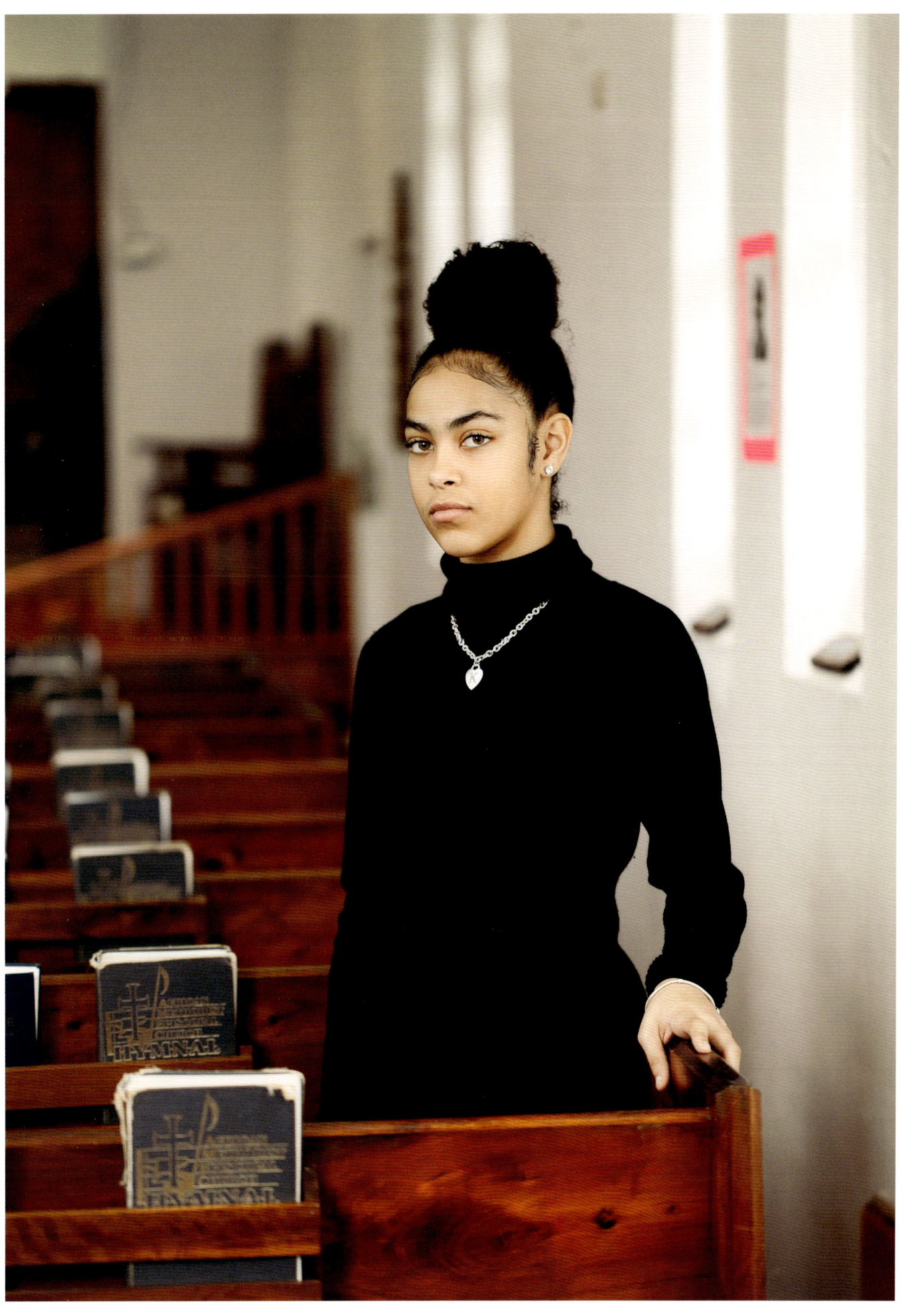

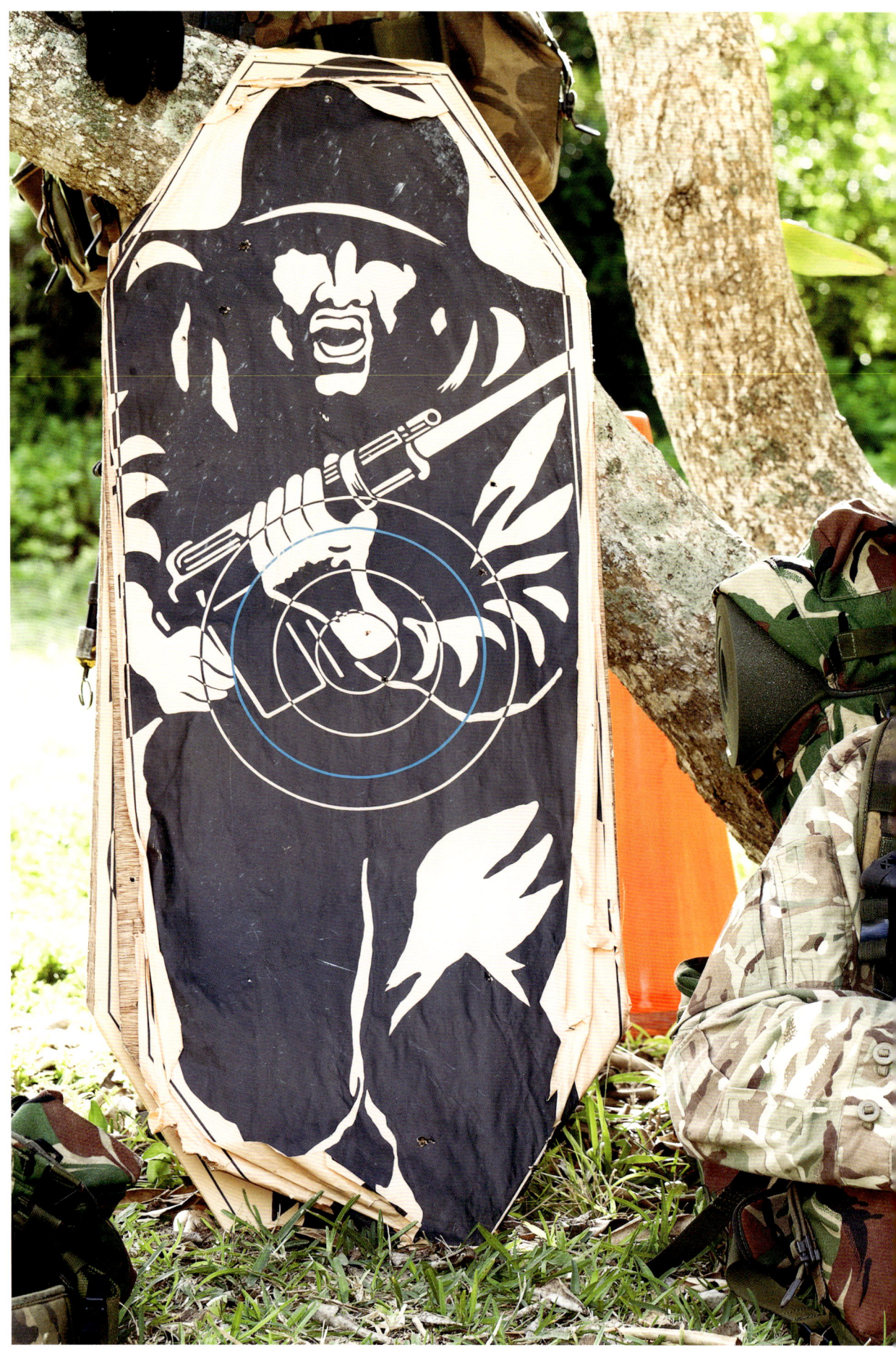

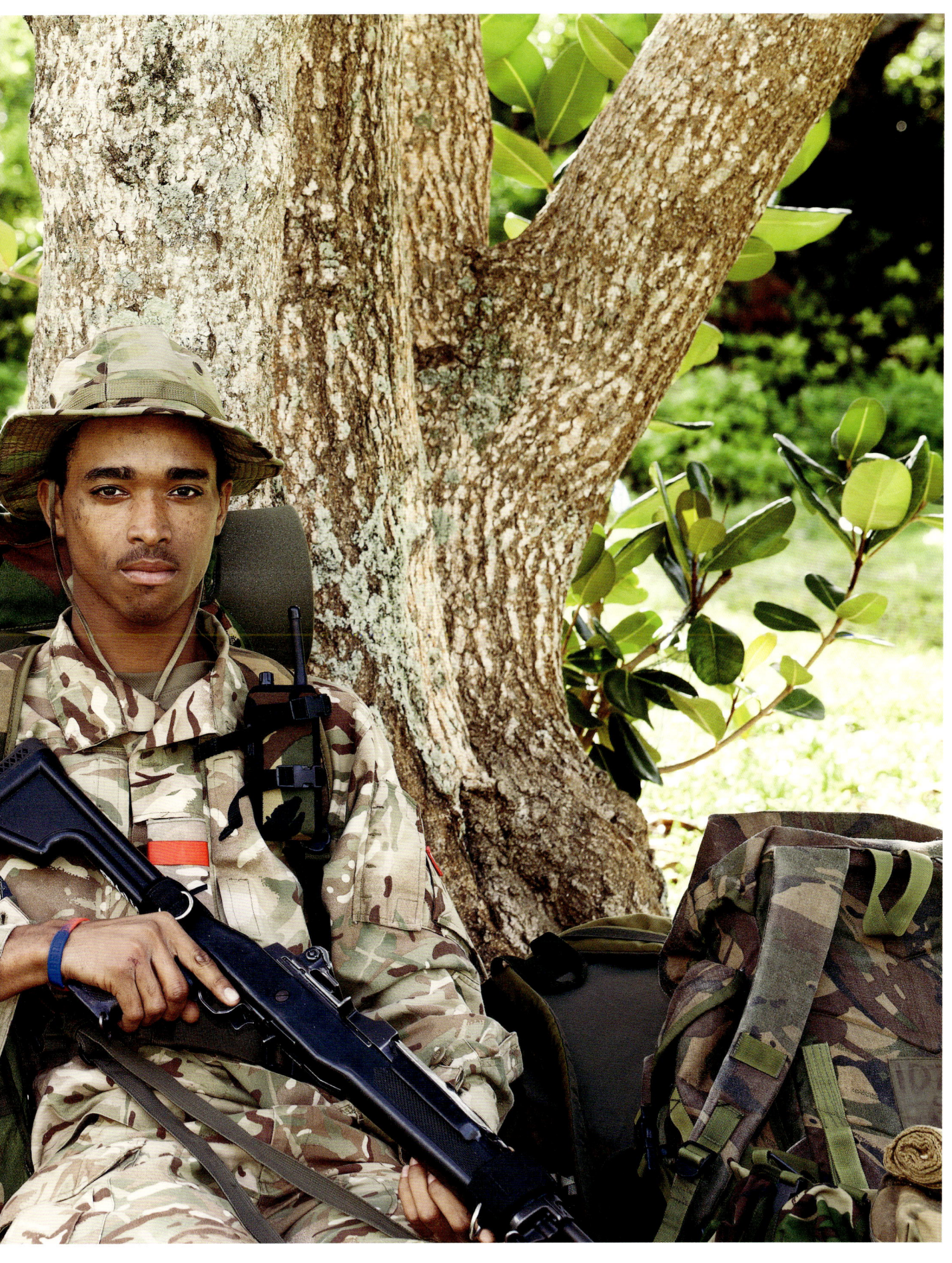

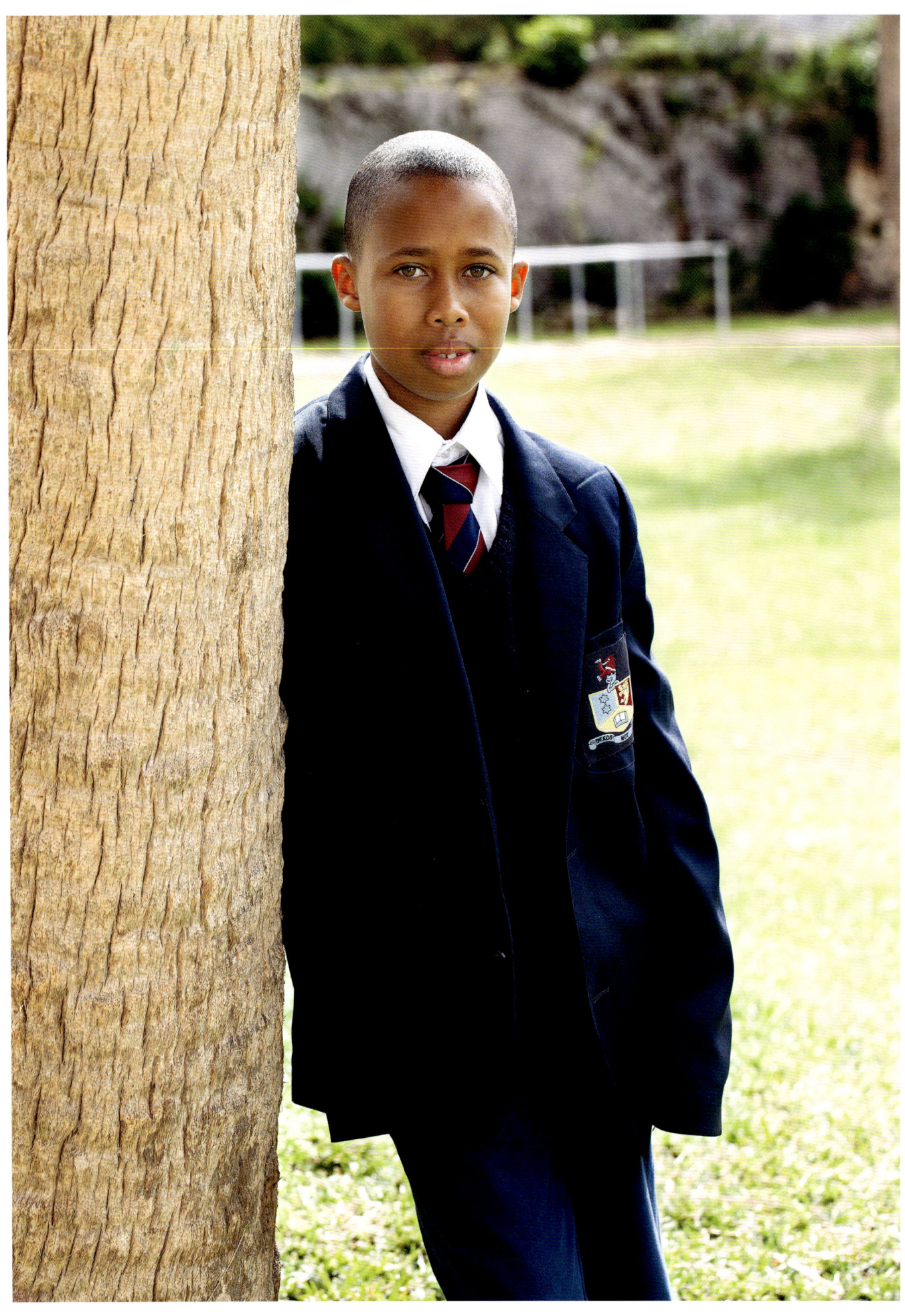

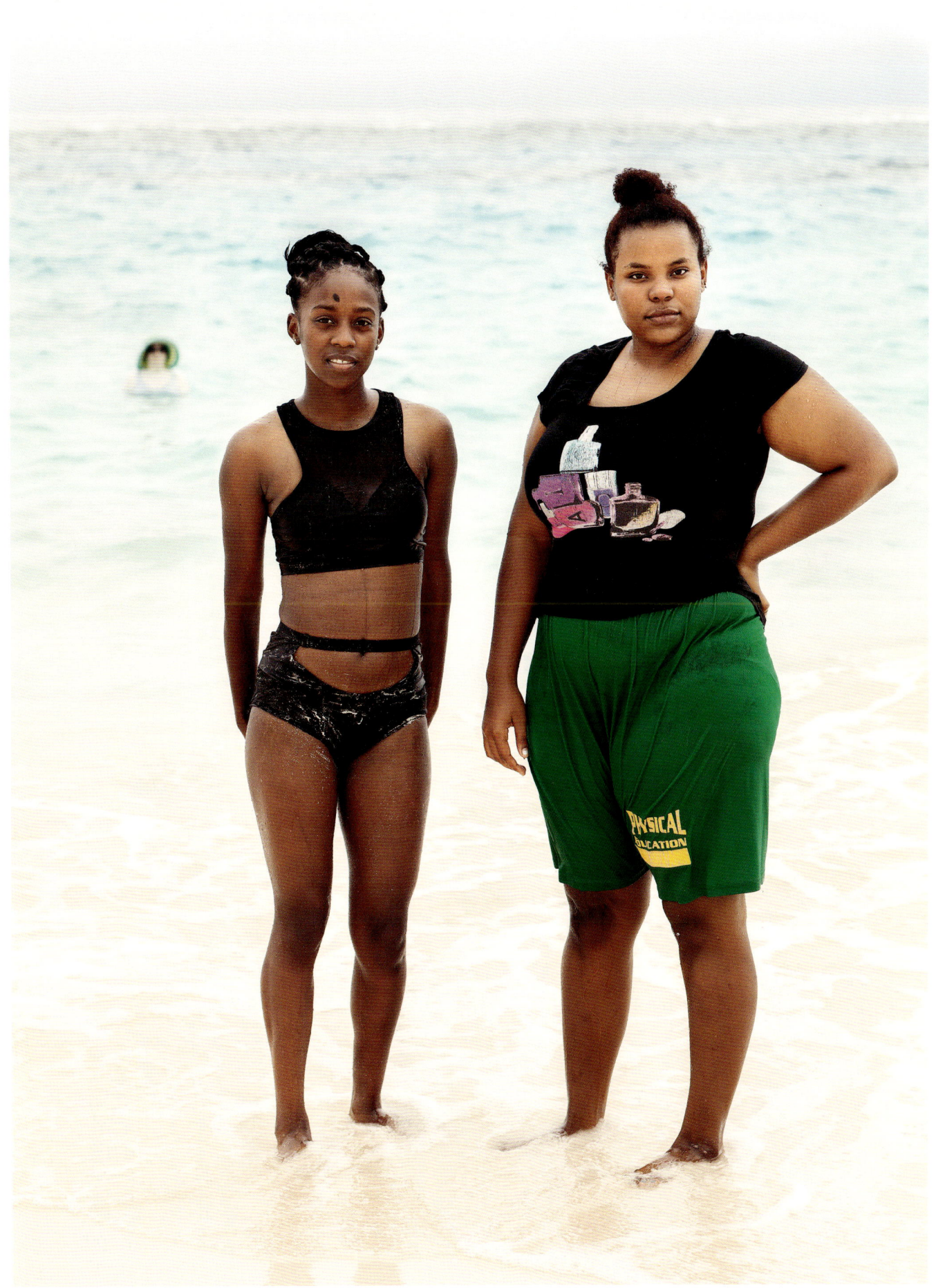

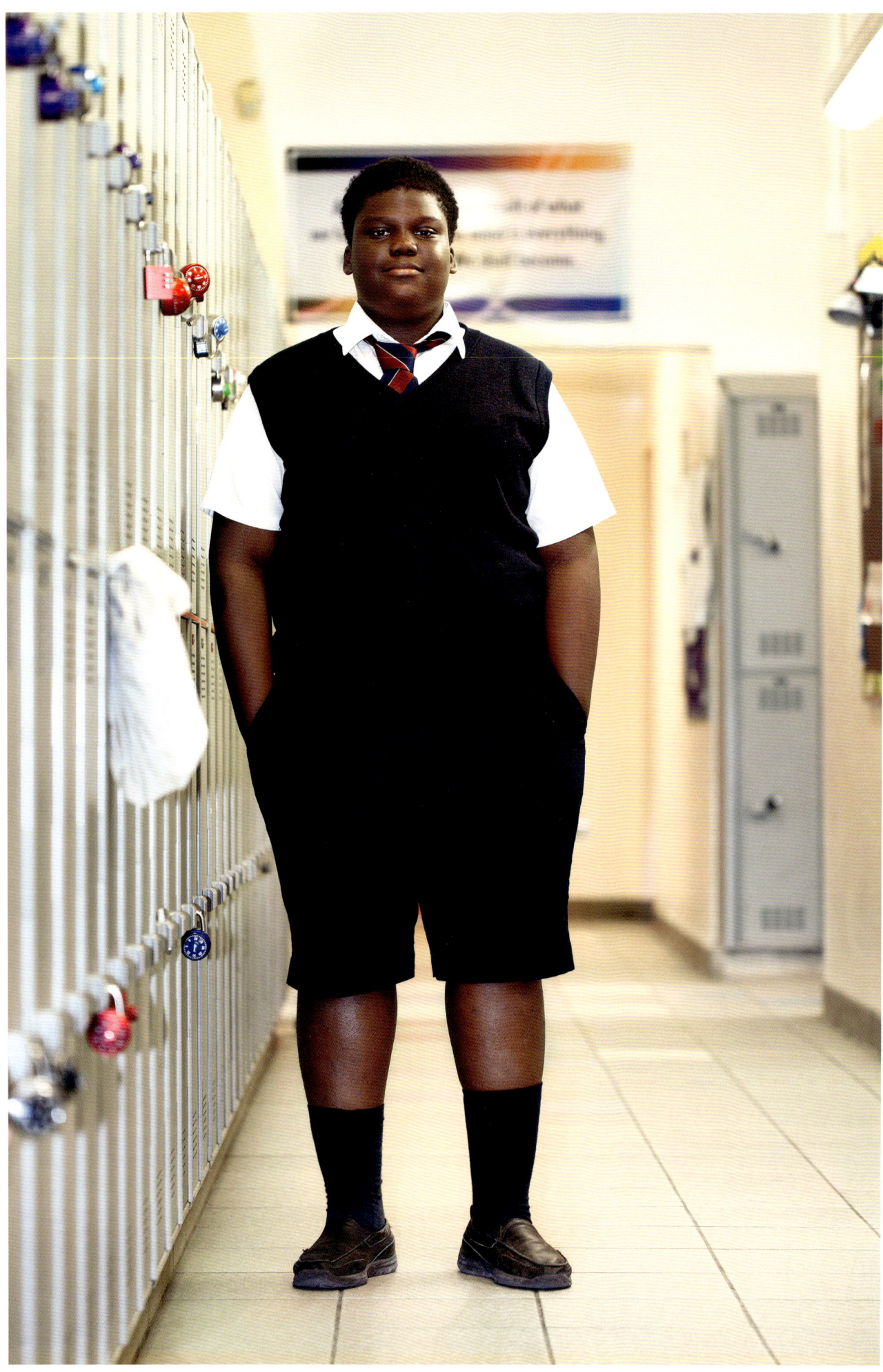

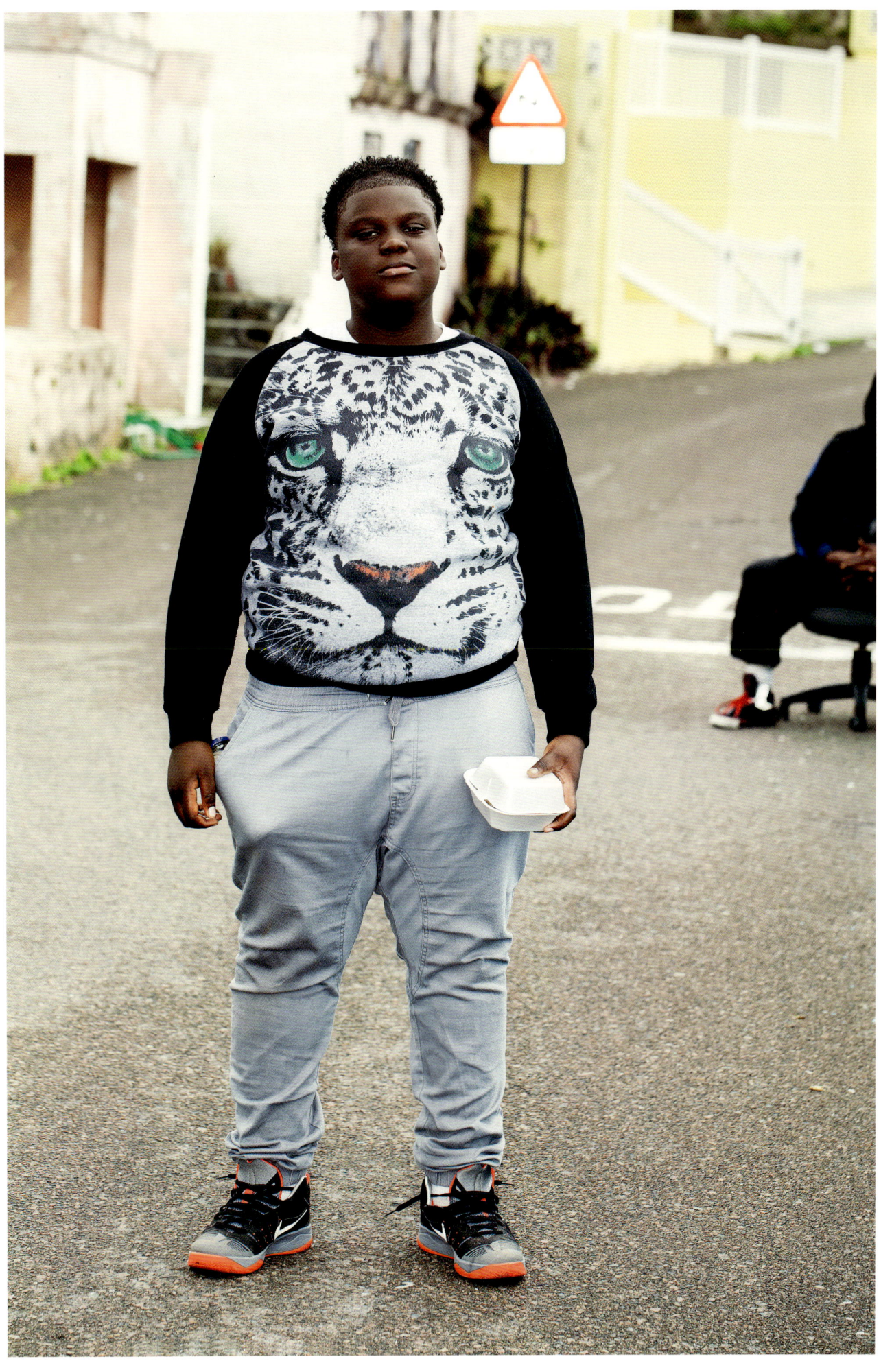

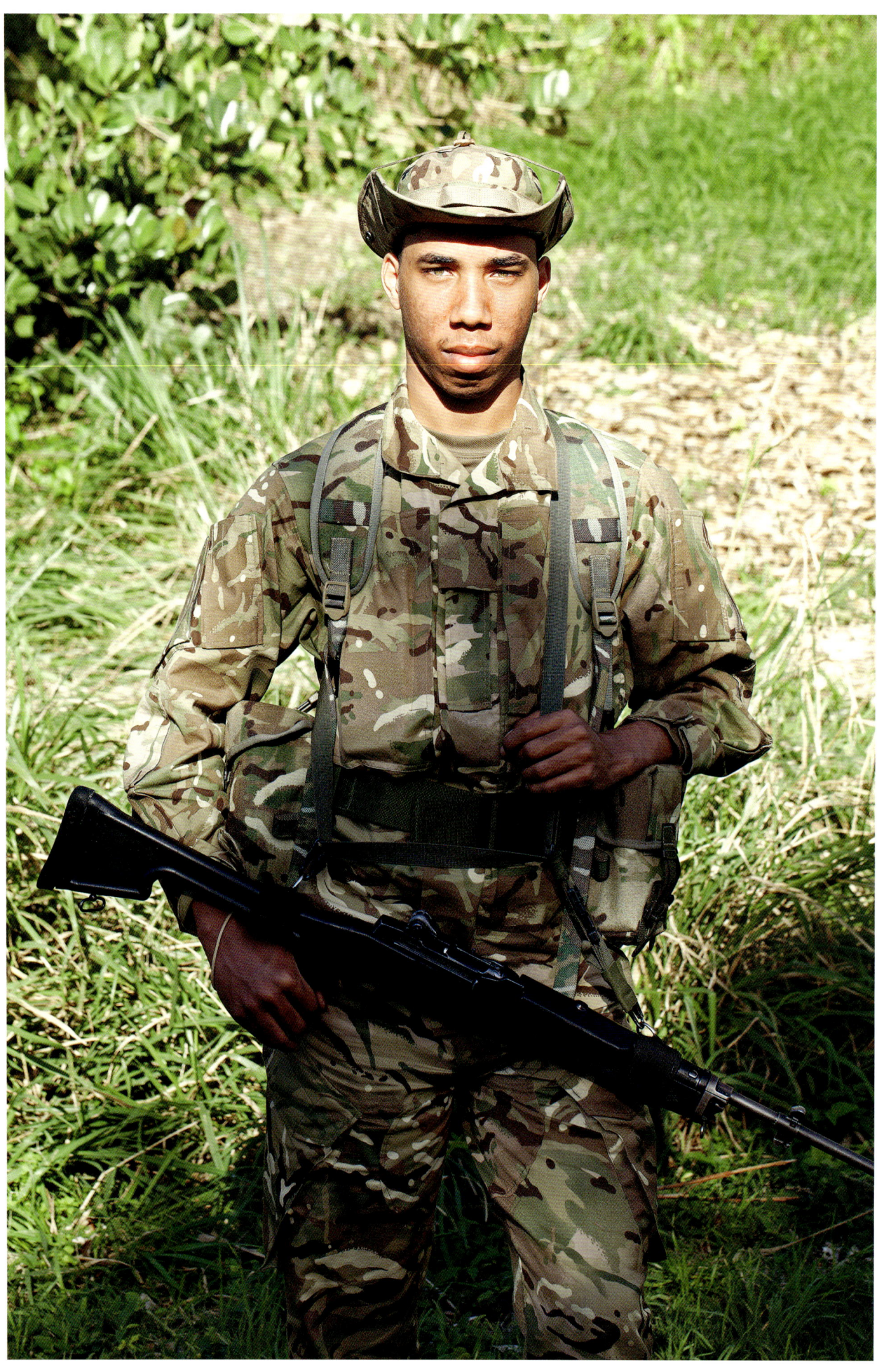

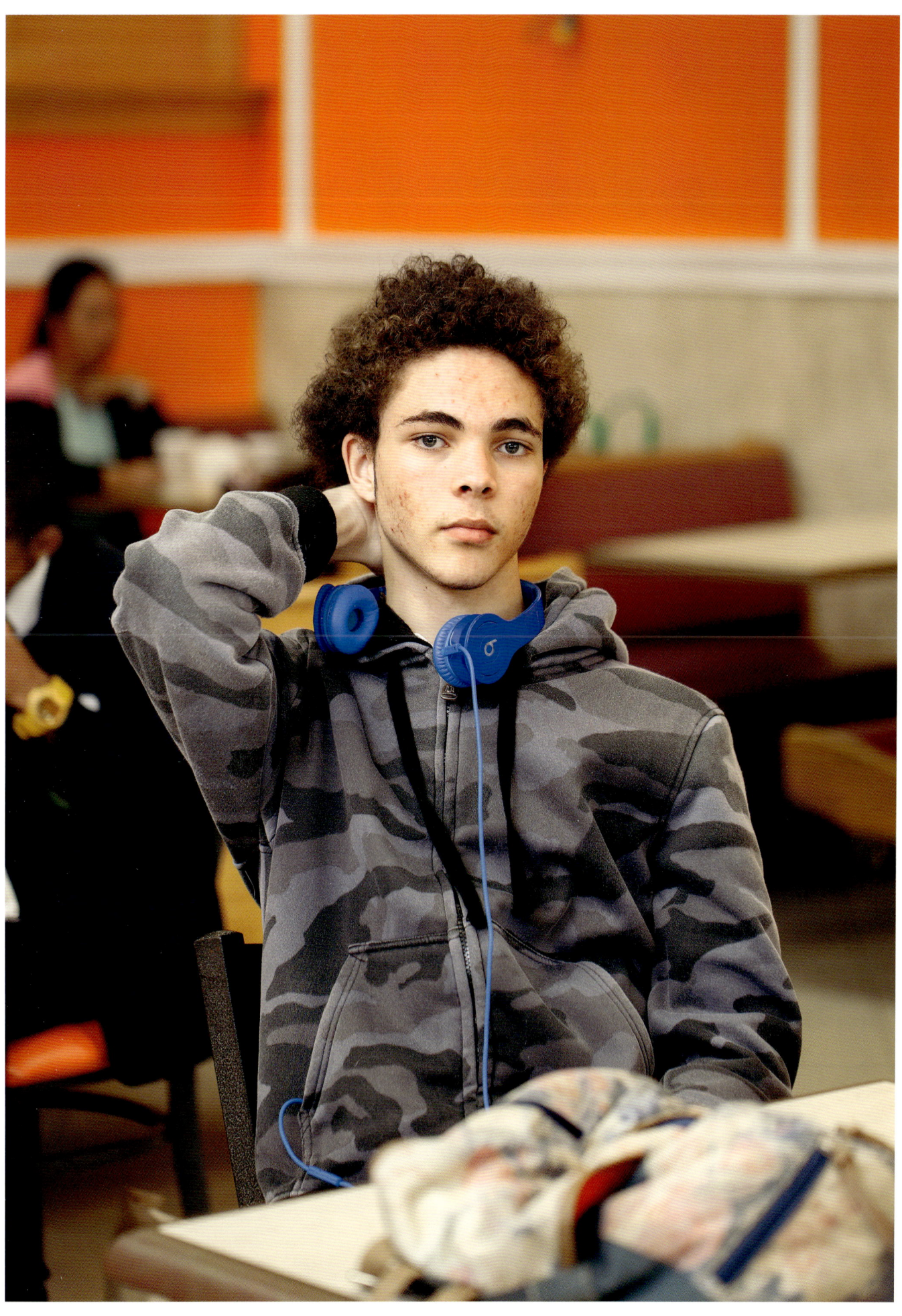

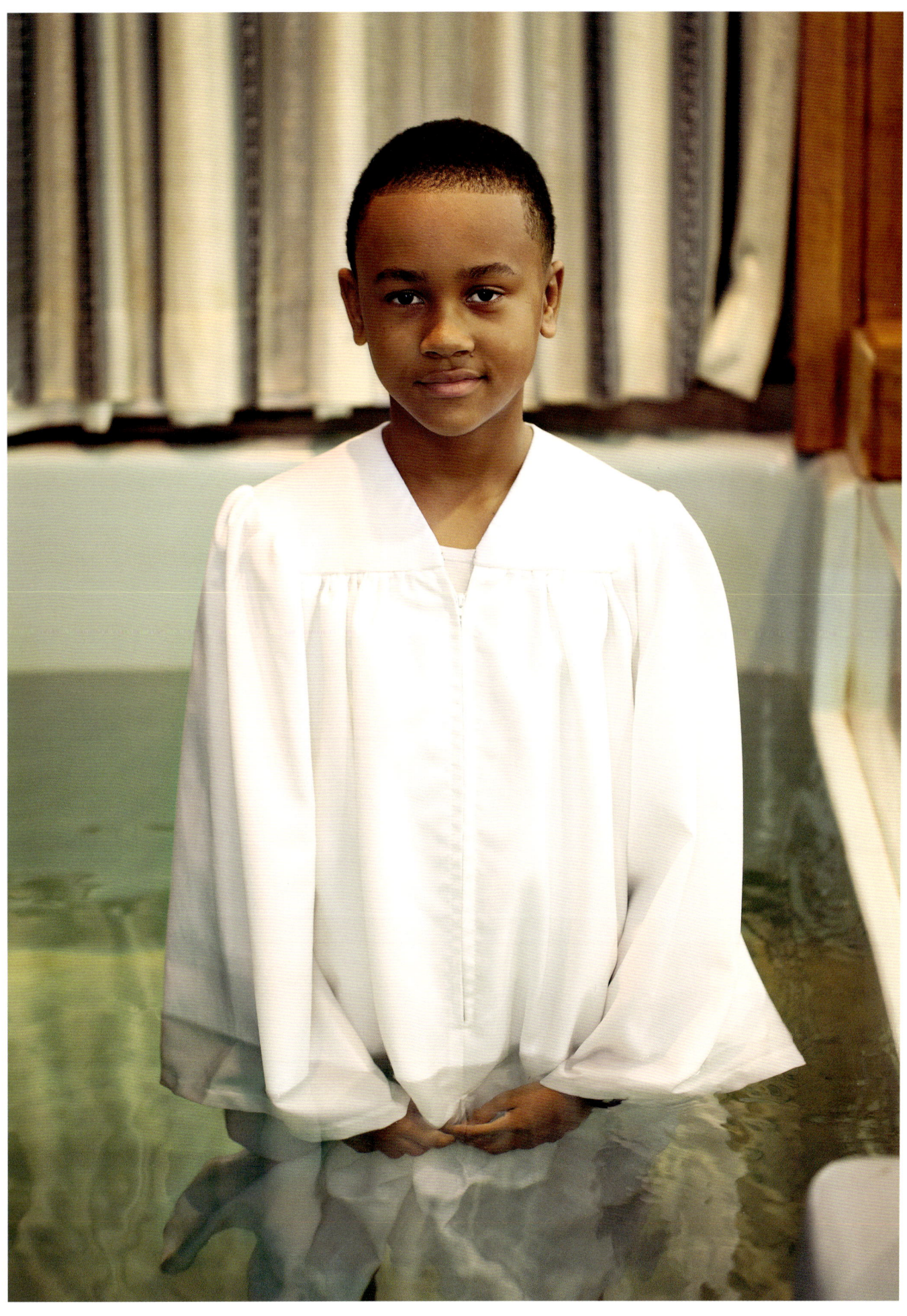

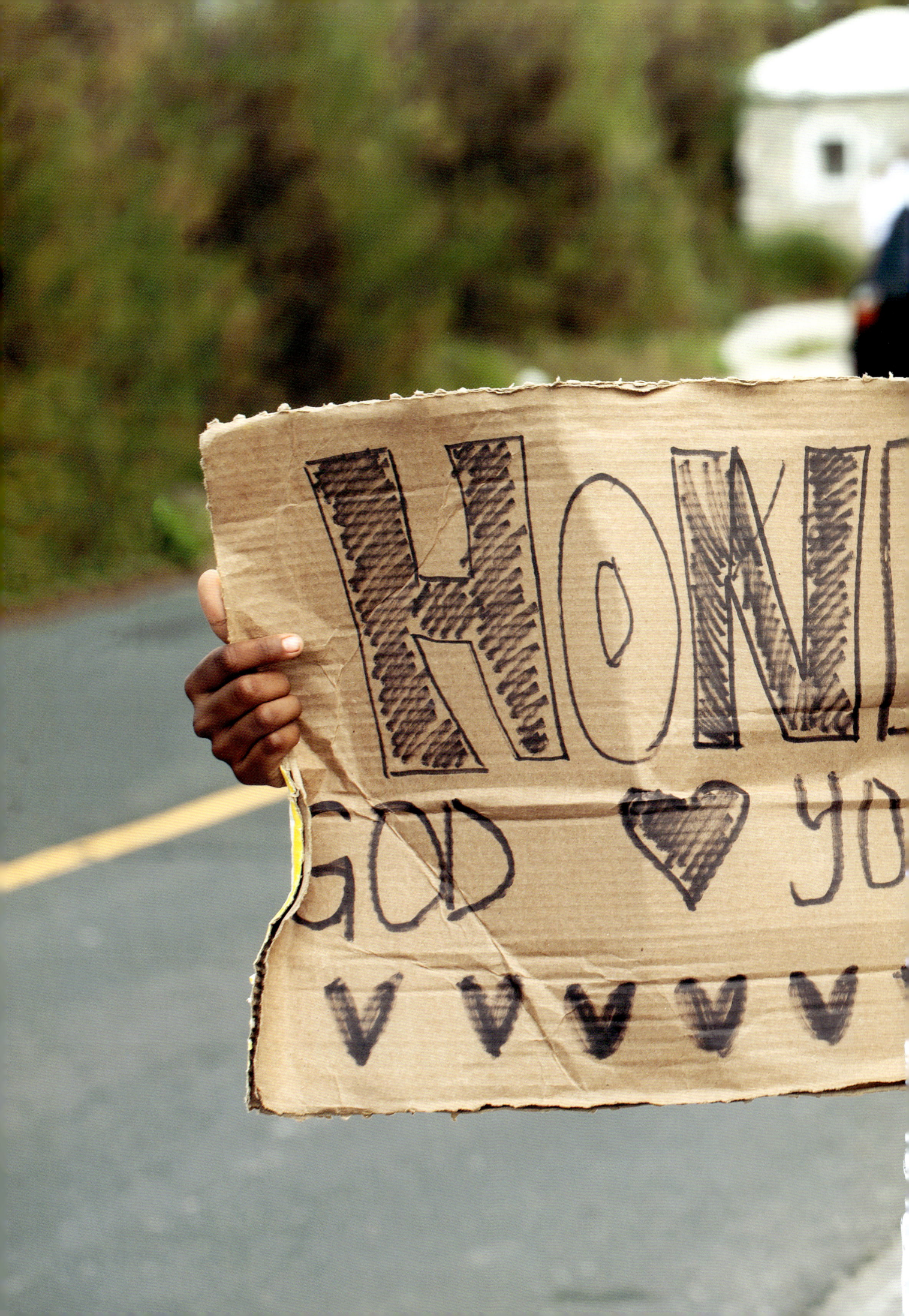

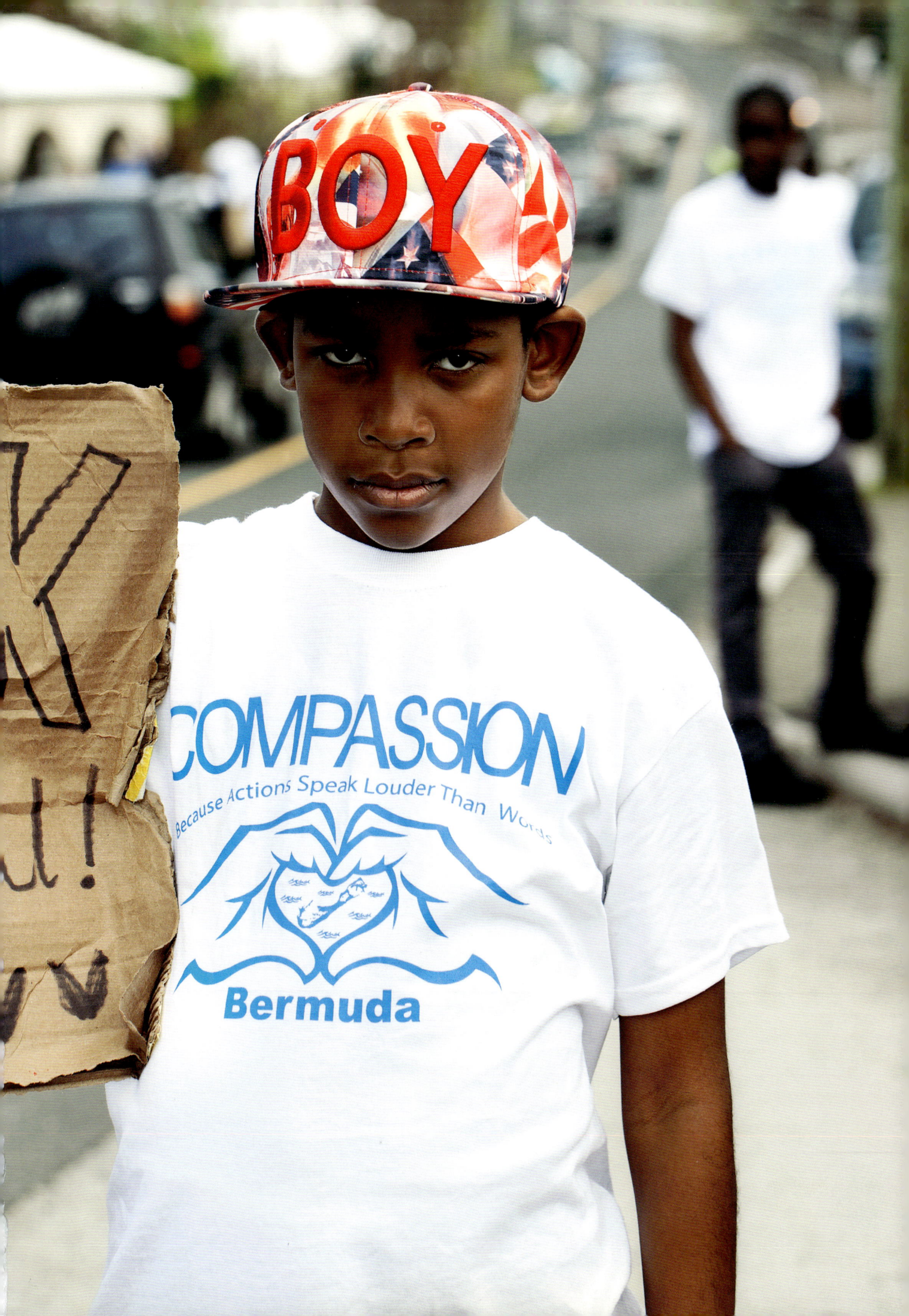

# THE HONOURABLE DAME PAMELA GORDON BANKS DBE, JP

If "the eyes are the window to the soul," then gaze with your own eyes on the faces that Debra Friedman has captured in her photographs, and you will begin to know who these teenagers are. Gaze further into their young eyes, and you'll know them better still. You'll see joy and tumult, hope and fear, all the contradictions that visit anyone caught in the most formative stage of life we know.

Our children come by contradictions honestly: their home is one of them. Bermuda is open and mysterious at once, an island that's also an invisible mountain, a mile-high mountain that happens to be mostly under water. Is there a more apt metaphor for adolescence? Open and mysterious at once, with more of its depth hidden than revealed?

It takes a special eye to plumb the complicated eyes of teenagers, to navigate the complex windows to their souls. Debra Friedman has just such an eye, and the talent to share what she sees through her extraordinary photography. Her images of Bermudian youth evoke the artistry of the legendary Alfred Eisenstaedt and Gordon Parks. It was a great stroke of inspiration that led Masterworks to invite Debra to travel from Canada to practice her art in Bermuda. And a great blessing that she accepted.

What does the photographer see that we can see now, too? That young people dance the dance of change every moment of every day. That each new day is a referendum on self-worth and doubt and promise. That our children are as familiar as our own skin, and as strange as visitors from another planet.

And finally, this: gaze once more at the beautifully simple images on these pages, and tell me if you see the thing I cannot escape:

The eyes have it.

DAME PAMELA GORDON BANKS was the first woman, and youngest person, ever to serve as the Premier of Bermuda. As head of state, Dame Pamela led a cabinet that fostered the continued growth of international business and educational advancement, during which Bermuda experienced unrivaled prosperity.

Knighted by Her Majesty, Queen Elizabeth II, for service to her country, Dame Pamela helped to unify Bermuda with Britain's other Overseas Territories and marshaled their representatives in negotiations with the UK government. Her years of public service brought Dame Pamela together with leaders as diverse as Benazir Bhutto, Fidel Castro, Eugenia Charles, Jean Chrétien, Hillary Clinton, Coretta Scott King, Margaret Thatcher, and John Major.

In more than 14 years in politics, Dame Pamela served in such varied positions as Premier, leader of the opposition, Minister of the Environment and Natural Resources, Minister of Youth and Sport, and Member of Parliament.

To promote responsible governance, Dame Pamela has debated politics everywhere from CNN to the Oxford Union to Harvard University's Kennedy School of Government to the Woodrow Wilson Center for Scholars. As a fellow of Harvard's Institute of Politics, Dame Pamela has extensively lectured university students keen to practice "the art of the possible."

Dame Pamela champions a vision of hope grounded in economic reality. She draws on the knowledge gained from earning her MBA at Queen's University to advocate her vision with fellow members of the Council of Women World Leaders and the Global Leaders of Tomorrow at the World Economic Forum.

Currently, Dame Pamela is actively involved with several international charitable organizations with a special focus on providing essential health care for some of the world's most impoverished people. In addition, she works continuously to provide scholarship aid for Bermudian students.

Married to Andrew Banks, Dame Pamela has four accomplished adult children and three beautiful grandchildren, and is blessed to live in Bermuda.

# THE MAKING OF MASTERWORKS AND THE ARTIST IN RESIDENCE PROGRAM

In the summer of 1987 I gathered together a group of Bermudians to help me realize an improbable dream. In the words of Rosemary Jones, in her definitive essay "Masterworks Legacy," our aim was to "repatriate and collect important works of art inspired by Bermuda and, by doing so, to encourage a more robust national understanding of local history and culture." And so, the Masterworks Foundation was formed.

If our aim was lofty, it was also overdue. It was our contention that as Bermudians, living in a place too often regarded as a geographical and historical afterthought, we needed to develop a deeper sense of who we were. It seemed clear to us that we could do that best by seeing ourselves through the eyes of outsiders: in particular, the remarkable contingent of important 20th-century artists who had come to Bermuda to paint and sometimes to live, people who had been inspired by the island and who had produced seminal works that now might hopefully show us to ourselves.

We began by establishing our collection with the purchase of a dozen pieces that we refer to as the "Twelve Apostles." These included works by Prosper Senat, Ogden Pleissner, Thomas Anshutz, and a pencil sketch titled *Bermuda*, by George Ault (a precursor of Ault's oil painting *St. George's Park*, which we would coincidentally acquire two decades later). But it was left to two paintings we secured in the early 1990s to touch the "lofty" part of our mission. The first was *Banyan Tree Trunk*, by Georgia O'Keeffe, who would eventually be described as the "Mother of American Modernism." The second, the clincher, was *Inland Water Bermuda*, by Winslow Homer, a landscape artist widely regarded as the greatest American painter of the 19th century. If calling our foundation Masterworks had once been grandiose, it no longer was. A masterwork was now ours, and it had put us on the art museum map.

Our next step seemed inevitable. We'd started by using the work of talented artists to draw people to view the Masterworks collection; why not use the collection to draw talented artists to the island to do their work? The Artist in Residence program was the result: artist "outsiders" would be invited for a three-month tenure to live and create on the island. Their visit would culminate in an exhibition and would also include the donation of one piece to the museum, a gift that would help us continue to develop our collection with new contemporary pieces.

We saw the Artist in Residence program (which began in 1997) as a chance to go "beyond the reef line": not simply a way to bring artists of all disciplines to our shores to provide their fresh perspectives, but also an opportunity to expose our local artists to artistic innovations developing overseas. It is a nonacademic program, one that's about not degrees or curricula, but the power of art.

Which brings us to Debra Friedman. Debra came to Bermuda in the winter of 2015 as an artist in residence, with a photographic project designed to address our community of young people, who too often fly under the radar of our attention. Debra was drawn to Bermuda's "British-ness" and the nuances of colonial island life. She found special those things we still do here that appear anachronistic to other, more "sophisticated" societies: our adherence to school uniforms, to dressing up for church all day Sunday, to patronizing lodges and social clubs—all part of the Bermuda mosaic that are integral to the first 20 years of a Bermudian's life.

Debra brought her own measure of specialness to the island. Over the past 20 years, we've hosted many artists in many different disciplines but, curiously, no one who was keen on tackling photographic portraiture—until this project. We're thrilled to see a representation of the island's teens, young people who can so often seem an invisible entity but who are in fact our future. To view a body of work that deals so purely and deftly with the uncertainty and joy, uneasiness and awe, of growing up is a treat.

— TOM BUTTERFIELD

# CONTRIBUTORS' BIOGRAPHIES

Author DEBRA FRIEDMAN is an established and internationally exhibited photographer and educator living in Toronto, Canada. She has a BFA from the School of the Museum of Fine Arts, Boston, and an MFA from the Chicago Art Institute. She is the recipient of numerous visual arts awards from the Polaroid Corporation, the Canada Council for the Arts, and the Ontario Arts Council and has enjoyed several artist's residencies, notably at the Hambidge Center in Rabun Gap, Georgia, and at Masterworks Museum of Bermuda Art. She lives in Toronto with her husband, Robert, and has three adult sons: Nathan, Joseph, and Eli.

PAUL ROTH is director of the Ryerson Image Centre in Toronto, Ontario. Previously, he was senior curator of photography and media arts at the Corcoran Gallery of Art in Washington, D.C.; executive director of the Richard Avedon Foundation in New York; and archivist of the Robert Frank Collection at the National Gallery of Art in Washington. Roth has helped realize numerous exhibitions and film programs, including *Scotiabank Photography Award 2014: Mark Ruwedel* (2015), *Edward Burtynsky: Oil* (2009), *Richard Avedon: Portraits of Power* (2008), *Sally Mann: What Remains* (2004), and *I...Dreaming: The Visionary Cinema of Stan Brakhage* (National Gallery of Art, 2002). He is author and co-editor of *Gordon Parks: Collected Works* (Steidl, 2012).

YESHA TOWNSEND is a writer and spoken word artist from Bermuda. She holds a bachelor's degree in music composition and is currently pursuing an MFA in creative writing from Hamline University in Minnesota. She has served as the education director for the Chewstick Foundation's youth poetry program Break the Chains. She has performed internationally and locally as a poet.

TOM BUTTERFIELD is founder and executive director of the Masterworks Museum of Bermuda Art. He graduated from Ryerson Polytechnical Institute in Toronto in 1976 and received a Canada Council Grant for photography before moving back to his homeland, Bermuda, in 1987. There, he started Masterworks Museum of Bermuda Art, based on the notion that if Winslow Homer and other world prominent artists came to the island to create work, many other visual artists may have been inspired by the island as well.

# ACKNOWLEDGMENTS

It's always said, but it is true, that so many components must come together to allow this kind of project to survive and thrive.

First of all, I am so grateful to Tom Butterfield for the invitation to come and explore Bermuda with eyes wide open. His imagination and ability to seek out support on my behalf are what allowed these pictures to live on in book form. It is my hope that this book will help shine a light on Masterworks and the innovative initiatives advanced by Tom. The unique Artist in Residence program at Masterworks promotes a long tradition of viewing Bermuda through the fresh vision of visiting artists, and it has allowed the Museum to add to a unique archive of historic and contemporary works that represent this beautiful and complex place.

Clearly, thanks must be paid to all of the wonderful, curious, generous young people who shared themselves with me and stood as they were, where they were, to create transformative depictions of their best, most iconic, selves.

For the wonderful essays created for this book, I want to thank Paul Roth for his incredibly thoughtful and generous interpretation of my work, and Yesha Townsend, who captured the essence of "teenage" in her brilliant lyric poem "Tao of the Bermudian Teenager." Thanks, too, to Pamela Gordon Banks, for her thoughtful and kind message. You are a true role model for the young people of Bermuda.

Several of these texts, including my own, were reviewed and honed by the keen editorial eye of the writer and journalist Jay Teitel.

Text and photographs are nothing without solid, clean, thoughtful design, and for that I have Kelsey Blackwell to thank, for helping to interpret my desire to represent these pictures in a form that would speak to the incredible palette of Bermuda without eclipsing the images. No small task. Thanks too to Ursula Damm, for her critical feedback and advice, and to all the folks at Daylight who wrangle photographers so well.

I also want to thank Kate Ross, who squired me about the island, fed me fish tacos, and knew that good things lay around each wild turn and treacherous corner.

I am so very grateful to Jim and Debbie Butterfield for their generous hospitality in providing me a wonderful refuge on a hill to which I could return after long days shooting and luxuriate in the incredible view from my garden.

I am also indebted to clever assistants who helped take my raw files and pull the pictures out of them. Ben Freedman, Claire Harvie, and Parker Kay, you are the best!

I want to express my appreciation for the generosity and moral support provided by the wonderful Karen Hendrick, who helped manage me and grabbed a few tigers by the tail to help bring the project and the Toronto exhibition to fruition.

And then thank you to so many others for so much help along the way: Todd Fox, Talisa Dyer, Neil Pilkington, George Butterfield, Patrick Calow, Chris Gauntlet, Diana Gilbert, Michelle Hill, Tony McWilliams, Richard Lee, Gareth Nokes, Leo Richardson, David and Sheila Semos, Alikas Smith, Joy Symonds, Jennie Watlington, Heather Wood, Ben Beasley, Lynette Albouy, Deborah Smith, Richard Lee, Lateef Trott, and Elise Outerbridge.

Finally, and mostly, I want to thank Andrew Banks, without whom this book would be only pie in the sky. Andrew, your support, your advice, your belief in this project are just simply why it is. Honestly, I can't thank you enough, but I will try.

— DEBRA FRIEDMAN

This publication has been supported by

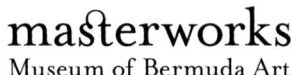

masterworks
Museum of Bermuda Art